Basic Metal Jewelry Techniques

A Masterclass

Carles Codina

Schiffer Publishing Ltd

4880 Lower Valley Road • Atglen, PA 19310

Published by Schiffer Publishing, Ltd.
4880 Lower Valley Road
Atglen, PA 19310
Phone: (610) 593-1777; Fax: (610) 593-2002
E-mail: Info@schifferbooks.com

For the largest selection of fine reference books on this and related subjects, please visit our website at
www.schifferbooks.com
You may also write for a free catalog.

This book may be purchased from the publisher.
Please try your bookstore first.

We are always looking for people to write books on new and related subjects. If you have an idea for a book, please contact us at
proposals@schifferbooks.com

Schiffer Books are available at special discounts for bulk purchases for sales promotions or premiums. Special editions, including personalized covers, corporate imprints, and excerpts can be created in large quantities for special needs. For more information contact the publisher.

In Europe, Schiffer books are distributed by
Bushwood Books
6 Marksbury Ave.
Kew Gardens
Surrey TW9 4JF England
Phone: 44 (0) 20 8392 8585; Fax: 44 (0) 20 8392 9876
E-mail: info@bushwoodbooks.co.uk
Website: www.bushwoodbooks.co.uk

Originally published Barcelona (Spain) Company of the Norma Press group of Latin America by Parramón Press, Inc. 2009 with the title of Jewelry Masterclass: Basic Techniques

Translation by Omicron Language Solutions, LLC

Library of Congress Control Number: 2013936598

Layout Design Adaptation by Mark David Bowyer
Type set in Eurostile

ISBN: 978-0-7643-4367-4
Printed in China

Carmen Amador. Pendant in silver and steel wire with aquamarine and magnetite.

Contents

Basic Knowledge

Techniques

Practical Examples

Introduction

Gold has been known and appreciated since ancient times. Due to the relative ease with which it is extracted from the ground, together with its malleability, color, and rarity, it started to be used as coins and as metal for ornamental use. Its resistance to oxidization and corrosion when in contact with the air ensures its longevity and allows it to be studied from various archeological remains. Working directly with precious metals allows us to get closer to the artisan processes used by ancient civilizations, understand their techniques and appreciate their value.

Both gold and silver, when melted down or mixed with other metals, such as copper, zinc, or palladium in varying proportions, undergo changes in their internal structure; they become harder or softer, their melting point increases, as does their conductivity, and they also change color. Due to their intrinsic characteristics, some of these metals are limited to purely ornamental use. The main aims of this book are to become acquainted with the various alloys, be familiar with how they behave, and adapt them to your creative needs, as well as get to know the various processes that are involved in the manipulation of metal (casting, fretwork, soldering, wire drawing, setting stones, etc.).

To my understanding, the art of gold and silver work is a very distinct discipline within metalwork. Therefore, it is unavoidable that the study of metalwork be combined with the aesthetic study of objects. By its very nature, then, this book, dedicated to metalwork with precious metals, must include some interesting and rather innovative visual ideas.

Carles Codina i Armengol

Abril Ribera and Roc Majoral.
Pluja collection.
18k gold earrings with rubies and black nylon wire.

Composition of alloys

It is crucial for all jewelers to know the concept of the composition of an alloy, as the manufacturing and buying and selling of precious metals are regulated by laws that require the fulfillment of a certain content of pure metal in an alloy.

The composition expresses the purity of the metal and corresponds to the quantity of pure metal contained by a certain alloy. In reality, this is nothing more than a numerical proportion whose numerator is the quantity of fine gold or fine silver and denominator is the total weight of the alloy of the precious metal. In practical terms, the important thing for a jeweler is the result of this division; that is, the composition of the alloy expressed in millesimal fineness.

$$\text{Alloy composition} = \frac{\text{Weight of fine metal}}{\text{Total weight of alloy}}$$

According to this proportion, pure or fine gold corresponds to 1.000 millesimal fineness, while the gold of 750 millesimal fineness is an indicator that it contains 750 parts fine gold and 250 parts alloy.

$$\frac{1000}{1000} = 1 \times 1000 = 1000 \text{ millesimal fineness}$$

$$\frac{750}{1000} = 0.750 \times 1000 = 750 \text{ millesimal fineness}$$

Multiply by a thousand to adapt it to the metric decimal system.

Millesimal fineness or carats

Gold and silver, like the other precious metals, are extracted in a virtually pure state through a process where the impurities are eliminated. What is known as fine gold is 1,000 millesimal fineness or 24 carats; fine silver is 1,000 millesimal fineness).

The composition of an alloy can be expressed in carats or in millesimal fineness; however, using millesimal fineness as the unit of measurements is much more precise and professional.

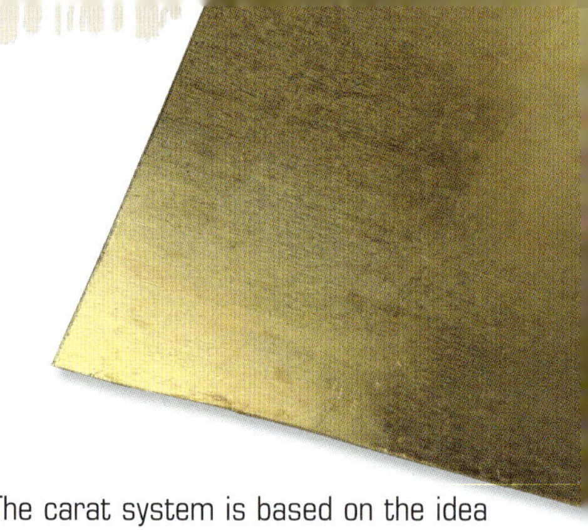

Fine silver is sold in the form of small granules of molten silver.

The carat system is based on the idea that a carat corresponds to a twenty-fourth part of pure gold. The millesimal fineness equivalent of 1 carat can be found by dividing 1000 millesimal fineness units by its equivalent, 24 carats. A carat, then, is 41.666 millesimal fineness units.

$$1 \text{ carat} = \frac{1.000 \text{ millesimal}}{24 \text{ carats}} = 41.666 \text{ thousandths}$$

Equivalence Between Carats and Millesimal Fineness

Carats	Thousandths
24	1.000
22	916
18	750
14	583
9	378
1	**41.6**

To find out the carats of a metal of 750 millesimal fineness, the millesimal fineness is divided by 41.6.

$$\text{Carats} = \frac{\text{millesimal fineness}}{41.6} = \frac{750}{41.6} = 18 \text{ carats}$$

Gold, like silver, is too soft in a pure state for making most pieces of jewelry. Therefore metals, mainly with copper and silver, are added to give strength and the desired coloration. In its pure state, it is obtained in the form of fine granules or in sheets.

$$\textbf{Composition} = \frac{\text{Weight of fine metal}}{\text{Fine Wgt} + \textbf{added alloy}}\ \frac{75}{75 + \mathbf{25}} \times 1000 = \mathbf{750} \text{ millesimal fineness}$$

$$\textbf{Composition} = \frac{\text{Weight of fine metal}}{\text{Fine Wgt} + \textbf{added alloy}}\ \frac{100}{100 + \mathbf{33.33}} \times 1000 = \mathbf{750} \text{ millesimal fineness}$$

Fine gold of 750 millesimal fineness

The gold alloy of 750 millesimal fineness or 18 carats is one of the alloys most often used for jewelry. In this alloy, each kilo of gold contains 750 grams of fine gold and 250 grams of an alloy of different metals. According to the metals that are used in these 250 grams of alloy, different metal alloys will be obtained (yellow gold, red gold, white gold, etc.), while maintaining the same proportion; that is, with the same composition of 750 millesimal fineness.

The gold alloy of 750 millesimal fineness or fine gold is possible if the composition is understood as a proportion (see formulas above). In all cases, the proportion, the important part, continues to be the same, which is why it is possible to prepare a final alloy of 100 grams of fine gold (750 millesimal fineness) by using 75 grams of fine gold and 25 grams of copper or silver as an alloy added to the gold. In the same way, if 100 grams of fine gold and 33.33 grams of copper or silver are put together this will produce 133.33 grams of gold of 750 millesimal fineness. These **33.33 grams** of alloy added to 100 grams of fine gold keep the same proportion or the same composition as the **25 grams** of alloy added to 75 grams of fine gold.

In practical terms, to obtain gold of 750 millesimal fineness, just multiply the 100 grams of fine gold, or the weight of fine gold to be melted, by 33.3 and divide the result by 100. Or, in other words, multiply the amount of fine gold by 1.33 to find the total of the alloy.

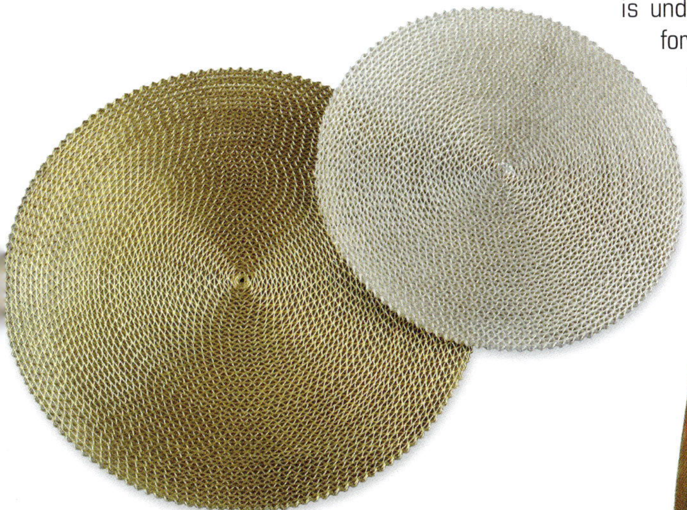

Liliana Guerreiro. Gold and silver brooches made with wire.

Enric Majoral. *Barquetes* Collection. Cuff of 18k gold foil and woolen strands.

How to find the composition of a gold alloy

Often, pieces for melting arrive at the workshop from difference sources, in the form of old rings, chains, or bracelets. It is useful to know their composition to correctly value them and it is necessary to regularly check the composition of a particular ingot once it has been melted, to ensure that it has kept the correct composition.

The most reliable method is a specialist laboratory analysis; it is inexpensive and the result, in millesimal fineness, is much more precise and professional than analysis with a touchstone. Analysis by an authorized laboratory is essential in order to officially check pieces made in gold, silver, or platinum. However, if you need to know the composition of a particular object and precision in millesimal fineness is not important, then a touchstone analysis is a quick and practical alternative. To do this, you will need a piece of gold with proven carats to set the standard. On a touchstone, first rub the sample that has proven composition and, right next to it, rub the piece with an unknown composition. Afterwards, put a drop of acid with a solution that corresponds to the known carats onto the samples and see what happens to the shine of the two parallel lines. If the unknown sample still shines, then the piece has a composition that is the same or higher than the known sample; if the shine on the line of the unknown metal sample diminishes, this indicates that the metal is less fine than the composition of the sample. If this is the case, the process has to be repeated with different solutions of acid, until you find one where the line maintains the same shine.

Make a line with a piece of 18k gold with a proven composition and, next to it, make another line with the ring with an unknown composition.

Apply 18k acid to the two samples and look at the shine; in this case, the shine is maintained, indicating that the gold of the piece is 18k.

If the shine of the sample diminishes, this indicates that its composition is less than 18k and, therefore, the test will have to be repeated using 14k acid.

To know the result of different carats, carry out the same process using acids of each of the carat compositions on the samples to be analyzed.

To analyze if an object is made of silver, just use it to make a line on the stone and apply the same 18k acid; a bluish reaction is an indicator that it is silver, but not pure silver. The acid contains nitric acid that reacts with the silver in the form of silver chloride.

Ana Cardim. **Pin made of plastic and paper.** With this piece the author questions the intrinsic value that up to now has been associated with metals and jewelry. Nowadays, there are examples of great artistic value made with the most unusual materials.

Fine silver of 925 millesimal fineness

Silver with a 925 composition is the most commonly used in jewelry. It is usually alloyed in a composition proportion of 925 millesimal fineness; that is, 925 parts of fine silver and 75 parts of copper (although, sometimes, other metals can be added to improve the color or mechanical properties).

$$\frac{\textbf{Weight of fine metal}}{\textbf{Fine Weight + added alloy}} = \frac{925}{925 + \mathbf{75}} \times 1000 = \textbf{925 millesimal fineness}$$

The formula shows that to make a composition of 925 millesimal fineness, 75 grams of copper must be added to 925 grams of fine silver to obtain the correct proportion. To obtain a silver alloy of 925 millesimal fineness from 100 grams of fine silver (1.000 millesimal fineness), the following formula is used:

$$\frac{100}{100 + 8.10} \times 1.000 = 925 \text{ millesimal fineness}$$

The 8.10 grams of copper keep the proportion of 925. Therefore, the added 75 millesimal fineness represent 8.10% of the 925 millesimal fineness of fine silver exactly.

Practically speaking, to obtain 925 fine silver, multiply the 100 grams, or the weight of the fine silver to be melted, by 8 and divide by 100. This simple percentage indicates the amount of alloy that needs to be added to the fine silver to obtain 925 marked silver.

Gold and silver

Gold

Gold, in a pure state, is a yellow metal that is not affected by atmospheric agents; it is very resistant to humidity and most corrosive chemical products, apart from some acids, such as royal water, a mixture of hydrochloric acid and nitric acid. It has a high density and is very malleable, especially in a pure state; it is a good conductor of electricity and heat. Its hardness improves considerably and it changes color with the addition of other metals, generally silver and copper.

18 carat gold

Yellow 18 carat gold, or gold of 750 millesimal fineness, is an alloy that often contains copper and silver in varying proportions. Adding a larger amount of copper than silver to the alloy results in it becoming harder and more reddish in color; on the other hand, an increase in the proportion of silver to the copper decreases its hardness and gives the metal a clearer, more yellowish tone. Nickel and zinc can also be used in a gold alloy; they give it increased hardness. It is advisable, though, only to use copper and silver to make yellow gold objects in a small or medium size workshop.

MOST COMMON YELLOW GOLD ALLOY OF 750 MILLESIMAL FINENESS

	% fine gold	% silver	% copper
straw yellow	75	12.5	12.5
red	75	62	18.8
green	75	18.8	62

The coloration of a hard, very red gold can be intensified by adding 25% copper. On the other hand, a green gold can be made more yellow, although also too soft, by adding 25% fine silver.

Carles Codina. Oxidized silver ring.

Liliana Guerreiro. Filigree rings in gold and silver.

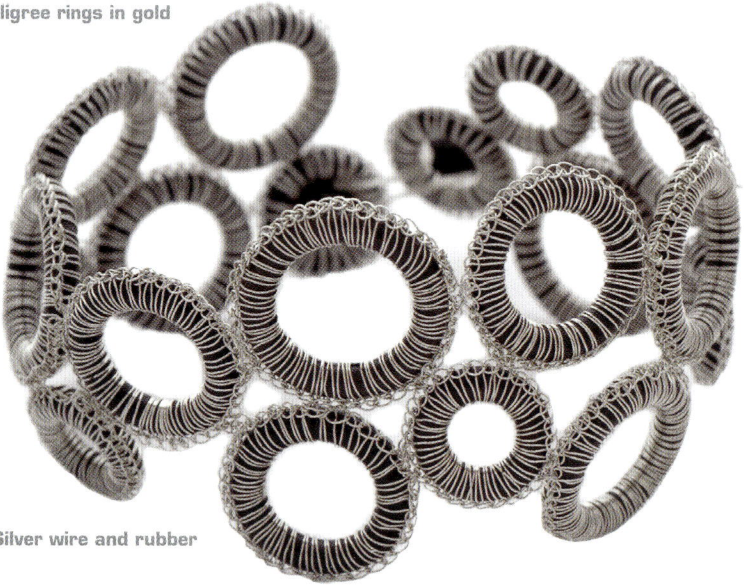

Inés Sobreira. Silver wire and rubber bracelet.

White gold

White gold is an alloy that must respect the same proportion as yellow, red, or green gold; that is, 750 parts fine gold and 250 parts alloy. The difference is that the 250 millesimal fineness contains different proportions of palladium, silver, or nickel. As palladium is a metal that melts at high temperatures, it is necessary to use oxygen to prepare the different alloys of palladium white gold. There are also various prepared alloys that do not require the use of oxygen when melted; these alloys do not generally contain palladium, which also reduces the final cost of the metal. Some contain nickel-zinc, making metal that is harder and stronger. The harder the metal the longer it lasts and the better preserved it is. A hard metal can be useful for making settings or prongs for gemstones, as well as for certain types of fine wire. However, the use of alloys brings about some issues regarding its reuse and the recasting of the leftover remnants, as well as its later recovery.

Stefano Marchetti. Ring made from various sheets of gold.

DIFFERENT ALLOYS OF PALLADIUM WHITE GOLD
(thousandths)

Gold	Paladium	Silver	Copper
750	125	125	
750	80	125	45
750	200	50	
750	250		

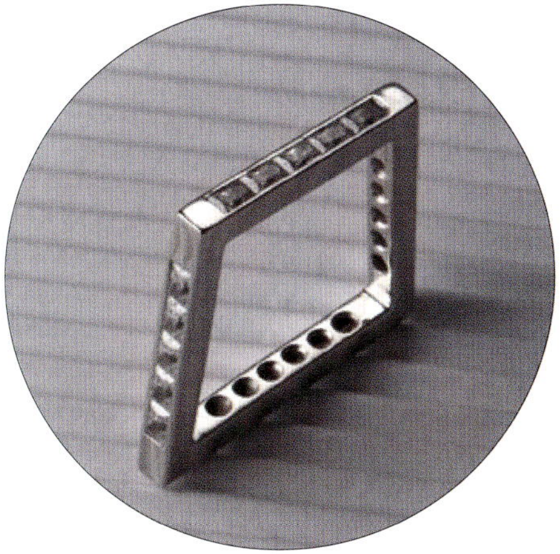

Dani Fàbregues. Princess cut diamond ring, in rhodium plated white gold.

Carles Codina. Cubes of yellow gold and white gold made from a 0.05 mm sheet, cut with a diamond.

Stefano Marchetti. Brooch made from gold.

Rhodium plating

White gold is not actually completely white; it has a very slight, very light yellowish tone, which is practically white, especially if the alloy has been made with palladium. To do this, an electrolytic plating of rhodium is applied once the piece has been finished and polished. Rhodium is an unalterable, very hard metal that gives uniformity of color and strength to a piece.

Silver

This white, shiny metal is very malleable in its pure state. It is an excellent conductor of heat and electricity, even more so than copper. It is extracted together with other minerals or as free silver. In a pure state it is unalterable and resistant to attacks by soda and caustic potash, but not to nitric acid, which creates silver nitrate, nor to products that contain sulfur, which makes black sulfur in the form of a patina. This is worth noting that the atmosphere contains a large amount of sulfur, which causes surface oxidization of silver, giving it a dark blackish tone. Silver alloys with almost all metals, except for nickel, iron, and cobalt, but the main metal used in the alloy for marked silver is copper. This hardens the silver without altering its color, if it is used in the right proportion and the right composition. An excess of copper can cause too much of a reddish color in the silver and an alteration in the composition.

Oxidization of silver

Silver tends to become darker over time when it comes in contact with certain environments (nitric acid, sulfuric acid, sulfur, hydrogen sulfide) or in contact with various emissions that contain small proportions of sulfur. All these cause oxidization and fading. At times, the jeweler oxidizes the silver intentionally by using potassium sulfate diluted in water and then heated. It is also possible to buy old silver patina directly from a supplier, as it is, in fact, the same product.

Burns or blue spots in silver

One of the problems caused by working with silver are what are known as burns or blue spots. These are marks, slightly purplish, appear on the surface due to the oxidization of the copper in the alloy. These burns can be prevented by melting in a controlled environment or atmosphere furnace, or by using an induction furnace; special alloys for silver can also be obtained that minimize this oxidization.

As a general rule, avoiding blue spots requires correct handling of silver in the workshop. The use of antioxidants that avoid direct contact with fire on the surface of the silver means that these blue spots will be less intense and, consequently, will be easier to eliminate with the grinder and polisher during the final phase of the finishing.

Akiko Kurihara. ***Night sky rings.*** **Rings made of oxidized silver and glass.**

Ulla & Martín Kaufmann. Yellow gold and palladium plated white gold rings.

Akiko Kurihara. *Ten.* Pendant made in oxidized silver and gold.

Luis Méndez. *Salamanca and Oriente.* Necklace made with different sized filigree gold wire balls and a Tahiti pearl.

Carles Codina. Rings of oxidized silver with details in gold.

Basic calculations and quick rules

Basic calculations

metal composition (T) = $\dfrac{\textbf{weight of fine metal (F)}}{\textbf{total weight of alloy (P)}}$

What do you want to know?	How can you find it out?	Examples
How to know the amount of fine gold contained in an alloy with a known composition	By multiplying the weight of the ingot (P) by its composition (T) and dividing it by 1000 (P T) / 1000 = F	If there is an alloy of 50 g of fine gold with a composition of 750 millesimal fineness and you want to know the amount of fine gold in this ingot, do the following calculation: (50 × 750) / 1000 = 37.5 g (of fine metal)
How to calculate what the composition (T) of an alloy of an ingot will be when the amount of fine gold that it contains is known	By dividing the weight of the fine metal (F) by the total weight of the alloy (P) and multiplying it by 1000 (F / P) x 1000 = T	If there is 22.5 g of pure gold (F) in a (30g) gold ingot (P) and you want calculate its composition (T), divide 22.5 by 30 and multiply the result by 1000 to express the composition in millesimal fineness: (22.5/30) × 1000 = 750 millesimal fineness This is, therefore, an alloy of marked gold.
How to calculate the final weight of an alloy that contains a known amount of fine gold	There is a quick rule for calculating the weight of alloy that a known amount of fine metal should have, simply divide this by the composition of the alloy	For 22.5g of fine gold (F), how much alloy will you use to make a composition (T) of 750 millesimal fineness? $\frac{\text{(F) 22.5}}{\text{(T) 750}} \times 1000$ = 30 g of alloy with 750 composition If you subtract the 22.5 g of fine gold from the 30 g of alloy, you will see that the alloy added to the fine metal will be 7.5 g.
How to prepare an alloy of a particular composition knowing the millesimal fineness of its alloy	By multiplying the amount of fine gold by the composition of each of the metals included in the alloy and dividing it by the general composition	To prepare an alloy of white gold with a 750 composition containing 80 thousandths silver, 125 thousandths palladium and 45 thousandths copper for 40 g of fine gold: 40 g × 125/750 millesimal fineness = 6.6g of palladium 40 g × 45/750 millesimal fineness = 2.4g of copper 40 g × 80/750 millesimal fineness = 4.2g of silver **Total = 13.2g of alloy** Do the calculation: $\frac{\text{(F) 40g of fine gold}}{\text{(T) 750}} \times 1000$ = **53.3**g of gold of 750 millesimal fineness 53.3 – 40 = 13.2g of alloy
How to calculate the weight of a model made in a different metal	By dividing the weight of the original model by the density of the metal, then multiplying this by the density of the metal of the original model	If you want to know how much a 12g piece of fine silver weighs in gold: $\frac{\text{12g (original mode)} \times \text{15.5 (density of the fine gold)}}{\text{10.5 (density of the fine silver)}}$ = 17.7 (desired weight)
How to reduce the composition of a particular ingot	By adding alloy to the ingot: (higher metal composition – alloyed metal composition) x weight of the ingot / alloyed metal composition = the alloy that has to be added	Reduce 25g of 22k or 916 millesimal fineness gold to 750 millesimal fineness. $\frac{(916 - 750) \times 25}{750} = \frac{4150}{750}$ = 5.53g of alloy the original 25g + 5.53g of added alloy = 30.5g ingot weight
How to increase the composition of a particular ingot	By adding fine gold to the ingot: (higher metal composition – alloyed metal composition) x ingot weight / 1000 – higher metal composition = grams of fine gold	If you want to increase the composition of a 5 g ingot with a composition of 650 millesimal fineness to a composition of 750 millesimal fineness: $\frac{(750 - 650) \times 5\text{g}}{1000 - 750}$ = 20g of fine gold to be added

Basic Knowledge	
To know the amount of fine gold in an alloy	Multiply the weight of the metal by 750, if it is 18k gold, and divide by 1000. The result will be fine gold
To know the final weight of the alloy from fine gold	Multiply the weight of the fine metal by 1000 and divide by the millesimal fineness of the alloy, 750 if it is 18k gold. The result is fine gold
To know the composition of an alloy that has a precise amount of fine gold	Divide the weight of the fine metal (F) by the total weight of the alloy (P) and multiply by 1000. (F/P) x 1000 = T
To calculate the alloy to be added to make gold with a composition of 750 millesimal fineness (18k)	Multiply the weight of fine metal by 1.333 or by 0.33, whichever is preferable. Example: with 75 g of fine gold, what will be the final weight of the ingot: **75 x 1.33 = 99.75 g of alloy** Example: with 75 g of fine gold, how much alloy is needed to achieve the total of the alloy: **75 x 0.33 = 24.75 g of alloy that will be added to the fine metal** The total weight will be: 75 + 24.75 = 99.75 g of 18k gold

Diego Bisso. **Silver, felt and permanent ink ring.**

Casting metal

Casting is an important process in the preparation of the various wires and plates that enable jewelers to make jewelry. It consists of increasing the temperature of the metal with the help of a furnace or the right welding torch, and, once it is in liquid form, putting it into a mold or cavity where it solidifies and takes on the shape of the mold. The molten metal can be poured into sand or heat-resistant molds, into charcoal, or into the most unlikely place to obtain a wide variety of shapes. This chapter explains how metal is cast in an ingot mold to prepare fine gold and silver in their two basic forms: wires and plates.

Temperatures

All metals have a particular casting temperature which has to be identified; it is also important to know how the metal behaves when in a liquid state, the correct types of flame for casting it and how to cool the metal.

Metal	Melting Point °C	Density	Composition
18k white gold	904	15.7	75 Au + 5 Cu + 15 Ni + 5 Zn
18k yellow gold	904	15.5	75 Au + 12.5 Cu + 12.5 Ag
14k yellow gold	802	13.4	58 Au + 25 Ag + 17 Cu
Palladium coated white gold	943	14.6	75 Au + Pt + Pd in different proportion

1/ Always melt the metal with the higher melting point first. For a fine gold alloy, first melt the fine gold,then the copper and the silver. For a silver-copper alloy, first melt the fine silver and then the electrolyte copper.

2/ Pour the metal carefully and continuously into an ingot mold that has been previously heated to avoid heat shock between the molten metal and the iron which would cause the metal to belch out of it.

Metal	Symbol	Density	Melting Point°C
Fine silver	Ag	10.5	961
Fine gold	Au	19.3	1,063
Platinum	Pt	21.4	1,769
Copper	Cu	8.9	1,083
Rhodium	Rh	12.1	1,970
Zinc	Zn	7.1	419
Palladium	Pd	12	1,552
Cadium	Cd	8.6	321
Steel	Fe	7.8	1,535
Lead	Pb	11.36	327
Sterling Silver	Ag + Cu	10.4	898
Tin	Sn	5.8	232
Nickel	Ni	8.9	1,455
Aluminum	Al	2.7	660
Brass	60 % Cu + 40 % Zn	8.4	940
Titanium	Ti	4.5	1,800

3/ When the metal has melted and been poured into an ingot mold of the right shape, either for wire or sheets, leave it to cool, then strip it in a bleaching solution in order to clean the remains of the flux that may have stuck to the ingot.

Flux

Melting silver is facilitated by the use of a flux. This acts by eliminating the oxides formed by the oxygen of the air generated during the heating of the metal; it also slightly increases the fusing point of the alloy when soldering or casting. The most common types are borax and its by-products, such as yellow solder, often used in jewelry, which is applied to the piece before soldering, protecting it from oxidization. The powdered flux, or purifier, is used to melt the metal and cleanse it of impurities during casting; it is poured into the crucible when casting.

Preparing the crucible

Crucibles are usually made from different types of refractory clay. Although it is also possible to cast in graphite crucibles, these are normally used in electric or induction furnaces to cast large quantities of metal. It is essential to prepare the heat-resistant crucibles before casting and to keep in mind that a separate crucible has to be used for each metal, as there is always a small amount of residue stuck to the wall which must not be mixed in.

To recover the crucible after using it for various castings, submerge it in a 20% solution of sulfuric acid to dissolve the flux and, in so doing, recover the metal stuck to the walls. Once it is dry, prepare it again as described previously.

1/ Prepare a white, heat resistant crucible for casting by melting borax or flux for metals inside it to protect it and stop the metal from directly sticking to the refractory crucible.

2/ Melt the flux in the crucible. Once it is in liquid form ensure that it is spread all over the surface, creating an even layer on the inside wall.

3/ The crucible is now prepared and ready for metal to be cast inside it.

Annealing and stripping

Annealing, cooling, and stripping the metal correctly are essential processes in all jewelry work, as they are repeated very often while making a piece. After heating the piece, it needs to be correctly cooled in order to solder or anneal it; this process generates surface oxidization which, if not eliminated, will hinder further work.

Annealing

This consists of heating the metal to a particular temperature for a set amount of time and then cooling it down. This is a crucial process that allows precious metals to be worked methodically and it has to be carried out numerous times by jewelers and gold and silver smiths while making pieces.

Metal hardens when it is being worked and it must be annealed to make the metal soft and malleable; if this process is not carried out, the metal cracks and eventually breaks. To work the metal again, its temperature must be heated to its annealing temperature using a gas torch or a furnace; the metal regains a crystalline structure close to the original and becomes malleable again.

Structure of precious metals

Gold and silver, at room temperature, are made up of a series of regularly ordered structures called crystals. When they are melted in the ingot mold, their internal structure changes, going from regular and ordered to unsystematic clusters, with the same order but in a different direction; as the metal cools more clusters are formed until they jostle against each other. When flattening, forging, or drawing the gold or silver, the spaces between the cluster structures are compressed, and, making a metal which is much harder. To recover its malleability in order to continue working on it, the metal must be annealed. When the temperature is increased, the metal recovers a structure close to that which it had originally, the spaces or displacements between the clusters increase, and a process of general reorganization takes place.

To anneal the metal, pass a low reducing flame over the object until it reaches a temperature of approximately 932 °F (500 °C); this application of heat is maintained for a few moments and then the object is left to rest on the metal part of the workbench or on the brick where it has been annealed.

Luis Méndez. **"Granulated button" set of signet ring and earrings made from 18k gold wire in filigree.**

Karim Oukid. **Filigree earrings in silver and enamel made according to the traditional technique used by the Kabyle people**

Forging, drawing, or pressing make metal that is harder and more compact, something that the jeweler sometimes does intentionally. A clear example includes the various types of clasps that need a hard and strong metal.

An 18k silver or gold ingot alloyed with copper and silver can be quickly cooled in water, after waiting some time for the temperature to decrease. Gold alloys can also be cooled in alcohol, which darkens the gold.

Cooling

After annealing or soldering a piece, it needs to cool, a process that also needs to be carried out carefully, as a sudden change of temperature can completely alter the shape of the piece. It is not advisable to cool it suddenly when it is almost finished or soldered with other elements, or when it is a flat sheet of metal, as the resulting heat shock can distort the object or the sheet. Direct cooling in acid should also be avoided because toxic gases are released and there is dangerous spattering. It is possible to cool gold alloyed with copper suddenly to soften it, especially for forging work. There is no fixed rule for cooling which is applicable to all alloys. The type of alloy has a definitive influence on cooling, which is why many gold alloys, particularly those made with an alloy that contains metals other than copper, can end up causing an effect opposite to that planned.

Gold of 750 millesimal fineness, alloyed with copper and silver in equal parts, and sterling silver alloyed with copper can soften if it is left to cool to 752 °F (400 °C) on the metal part of the workbench and then suddenly dipped in water.

Stripping

All annealing or soldering processes cause black oxide to appear on the surface of a piece. This surface copper oxide must be removed by using the right stripping or bleaching solution. The removal of this copper will leave a bleached surface in the case of silver, or an intense yellow in the case of gold, which can be reduced. There are various ways of doing this, one of which consists of rubbing the surface with a wire brush and powder from a pumice stone. Nowadays, there are various products specifically designed to strip gold and silver; they are much less dangerous than acid, do not cause burns, and produce less oxidization in the environment. In any case, the technical data sheets provided by the manufacturer should be consulted and the temperatures adjusted to those indicated.

Nowadays, products are made that remove the oxide efficiently and are less dangerous than sulfuric acid. They work best at a particular temperature, so a heater like the one in the picture is needed.

Cast ring after being soldered and stripped with stripping solution.

Acid or stripping solutions need to be kept at the same temperature and in a well ventilated place. Steel should not be put into them. To manipulate the metal use wooden, plastic, or anti-acid tongs.

To anneal coils of wire evenly, the wire should be rolled up and placed inside a furnace which is programmed to the annealing temperature.

1/ All mechanical work causes the metal to harden; the application of heat during the annealing or soldering process causes surface oxidization, which must be removed.

2/ Once the oxide has been removed, the surface has a white appearance if it is silver, or, in the case of gold, a more yellowish color; this is due to the formation of a very thin surface coat of fine silver or fine gold which must be removed.

3/ To remove this fine layer of metal, a scourer or course bristle brush and pumice stone can be used, or a rubber scourer and file can also be useful. The metal is now soft and ready to be worked on.

Main Stripping Solution

Stripping solution	Metal	Process	Safety Measures
10 to 15% sulfuric acid solution	Silver, Copper, Tin, Bronze	Always pour the acid into cold water, never the other way around. Then heat it. Not following this order will result in a dangerous reaction. Strip and rinse in bicarbonate and water.	Use antacids gloves, goggles and a protective mask to avoid burns. Always work in a ventilated area, since acid emits noxious fumes. 
20% potassium alum solution	Silver, Copper, Tin	Dilute the alum in water and then heat.	
Solution of one part nitric acid and nineteen parts water	Gold	Strip and rinse in bicarbonate and water.	
Solution of one part hydrochloric acid and three parts water	Gold	Strip and rinse in bicarbonate and water.	
Solution of nitric acid and water in equal parts	Bronze	Dip the piece into the solution carefully and quickly as the nitric acid attacks the bronze if left in contact too long. Strip and rinse in bicarbonate and water.	

Caring for and recovering metal

Working with precious metals requires some care; a meticulous approach is needed to avoid contact with those metals that, due to their structure, can have their behavior altered. Dirty crucibles must not be used and contact with lead, solder, and aluminum must be avoided as they can taint a gold alloy if they are introduced into it and turn it into a non-malleable metal that has to be refined again.

Great care also needs to be taken when recasting remnants with unknown alloy content collected from the workbench or workshop.

Refining gold by quartering

Often, pieces of gold from different sources have to be recast to create a new object. For it to be refined correctly, it is advisable to take it to a specialist company that will produce a metal of maximum purity and known composition. However, refining by quartering is still a useful procedure in a small workshop. The quartering process cleans the metal of impurities, leaving just the fine gold contained in the alloy. It is difficult to achieve a purity of 1000 millesimal fineness in fine metal; therefore, it is advisable to add 32% of new fine metal to the mixture to be certain that the gold obtained is 18 carat or 750 millesimal fineness.

1/ To obtain an 18k piece from pieces of the same composition, quarter them and leave in nitric acid for 12 hours to remove soldering. After rinsing, they can be cast straight away. To do this, take a piece of the gold and melt it together with four parts of electrolyte copper.

2/ The molten metal is poured into an ingot mold.

3/ The new alloy is stripped in acid and cleaned.

4/ Flatten in the rolling mill and cut into pieces of approximately 1 cm.

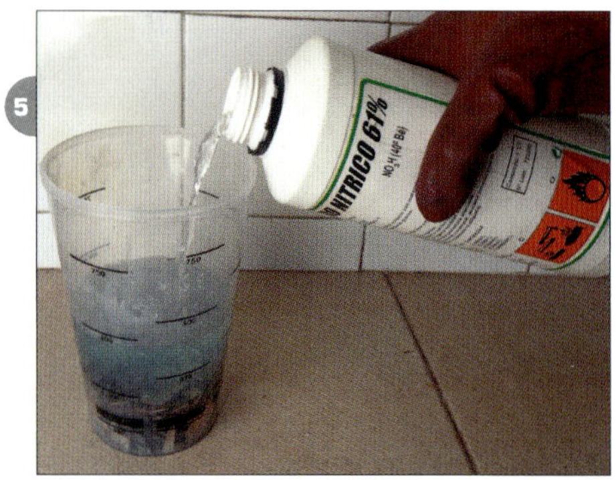

5/ Put the metal in a large container and treat it with nitric acid and a little water. Slowly pour in the acid while the metal is starting to react. At intervals, pour in more acid until there are no more signs of reaction. Leave it to rest for a few hours, then clean thoroughly with water.

6/ Filter the resulting metal through thick filter paper and leave to dry. Once dry, fine gold in the form of yellow powder will remain.

7/ Mix the metal with bicarbonate of soda and flux in equal parts, then pour into the crucible for casting.

8/ Once cast, a new ingot of fine gold will be obtained that must be alloyed to 32% to obtain 18k gold again.

Melting down filings

It is normal to have to melt down gold or silver filings and, often, this metal is dirty when it is collected from the work bench drawer. To recover this metal, it is advisable to keep the silver alloys and the gold and silver solder from fine gold, and to keep fine silver and gold alloys separate when working. It is also a good idea to clean the drawer and tools each time the metal on the work bench is changed.

When changing the metal or when finishing a job, the leftover filings and remnants must be collected from the workbench and cleaned before they are melted down again.

1/ First pass a magnet over the tools to remove the iron that has come off them. Then heat the filings in a pan to remove remnants of wood, wax paper, and other elements that are likely to have been burnt with the soldering iron.

2/ Put the filings in nitric acid with a little water; the acid will remove the silver, the copper, and the remnants of iron which have not already been removed and only the gold will remain.

3/ After rinsing in water and drying, mix with bicarbonate and flux in equal parts and put them in a clean crucible to obtain 18k gold again, if the filings have the same composition. If they have different compositions, it is better to quarter or have them recovered by a specialist company.

Sawing and fretwork

Sawing and fretwork are two essential processes which allow designs or shapes to be cut in metal with great precision. The main tool is the hand-held hacksaw, which is crucial for undertaking more precise work. This has various steel serrated blades stretched taut; there are different thicknesses according to the sheet or rail being cut. As a general rule, the thicker the metal, the larger the teeth of the blade being used.

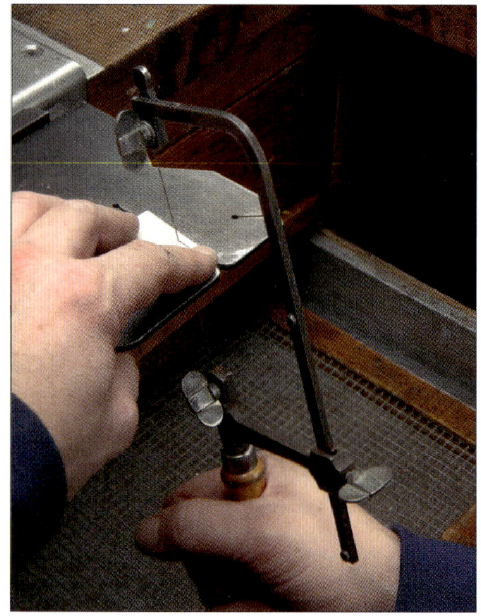

Process

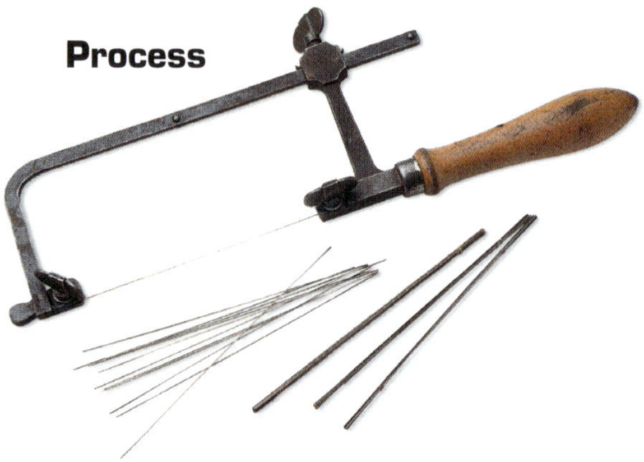

The hacksaw blade must be held taut by the frame of the saw in such a way that the teeth are facing downwards. Push the blade firmly into the lower part of the frame and slightly tighten it by pressing the upper part of the blade.

Once the frame of the saw is facing the right way, it can be used to cut normally.

The cut is produced by moving the frame with the taut blade downwards, in a movement that must be regular and precise, ensuring as much of the blade as possible comes into contact with the metal. At the corner, continue with the up and down movement, pivoting on the same point, and turning the frame of the saw before resuming cutting the next part.

To do inner fretwork push the blade through a hole cut beforehand with a drill bit designed for making vertical cuts, which is fitted to an electric motor.

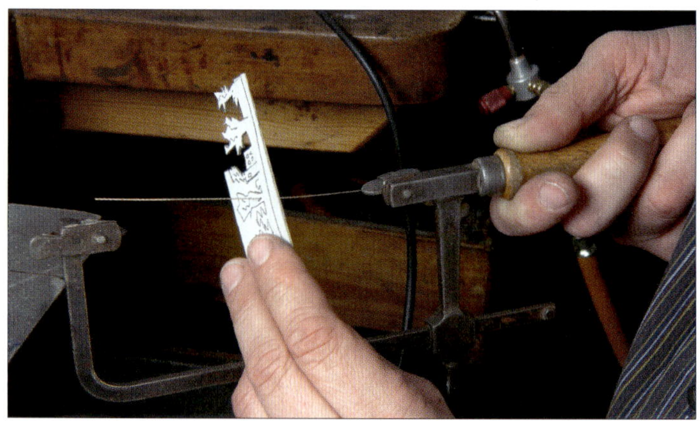

Then, insert the blade through the hole, tighten it and continue with the fretwork.

Simple Ring

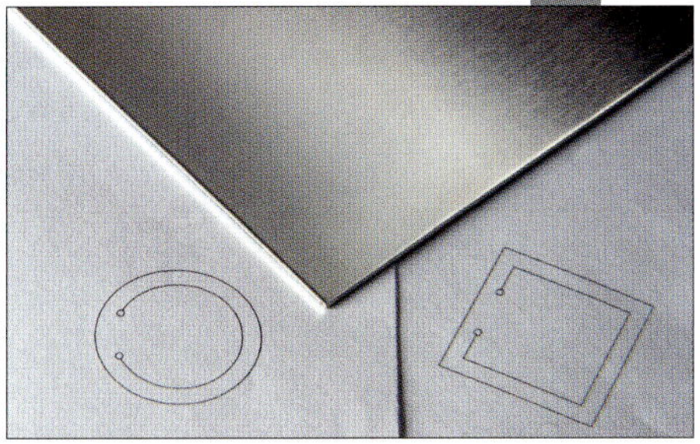

1/ To start cutting a sheet of silver, it is essential to begin with a perfectly drawn design. At times, the design can be affixed on the surface of the metal with white glue, or, if the design allows, it can also be drawn directly on the silver plate.

2/ To draw a precise line directly onto the metal, scratch the silver plate with a punch or any sharp steel tool.

3/ To do inner fretwork, make a hole in the metal sheet with a drill bit, 1.02 mm in this case. For this job, the size of the holes are bigger than the size of the saw cut, as they also have to allow for the inside of the ring to be bent.

4/ Once the saw blade has been inserted into the line, the inside is carefully cut, and then all of the outside.

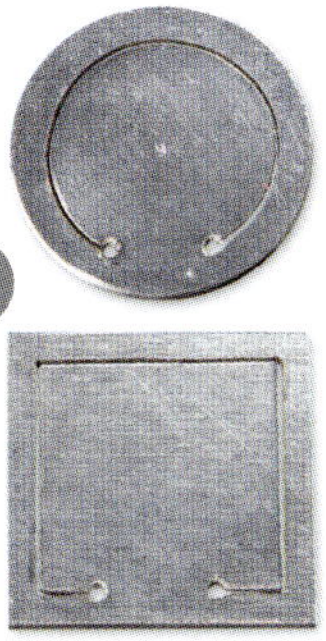

5/ With a fine file, go around the outside of the ring and the inner square to file away small imperfections produced by the keyhole work.

6/ Using parallel pliers, fold the inside piece until it is at a right angle.

Another type of ring made with the same technique.

Cutting discs

There are cutting tools that allow certain basic shapes, such as circles or squares, to be cut without using a hacksaw. Cuts with varied shapes can also be cut manually. These tools are very useful, as they allow for the same shape to be repeated quickly and precisely.

To cut an outline with these tools, a sheet of metal is placed in the inner slot of the tool and a cylindrical cutter placed in the corresponding hole. A single, even and precise blow with a heavy mallet will push the shape out.

Filing, beveling, and sanding

Filing and sanding are two vital processes for any jewelry work. Carrying them out correctly requires time and experience in order to achieve a good final result. Both filing and sanding aim to correct imperfections and reduce them to a minimum, enabling the piece to be polished. In general, filing is done first and then sanding, using different grades of emery paper.

For some hard to reach places it is better to cut a small piece of emery paper and roll it directly around small files with different surfaces to facilitate access.

Tempered steel **files.**

Filing

One of the most important processes for working with precious metals is undertaken with an extremely simple tool: the file. This requires skill, precision and control, and is crucial when making any piece of jewelry. Files are tools made of tempered steel which generally have two sets of very small notches, or teeth, that produce multiple cuts. There are different sizes and shapes, and various grades, which allow all corners to be reached and ensure correct filing. It is very important to have a good selection of files to achieve the desired effect with the metal, as well as for the finish of the piece. Files are very versatile tools which can be used to obtain very interesting textures and incredible effects on the finish of the pieces.

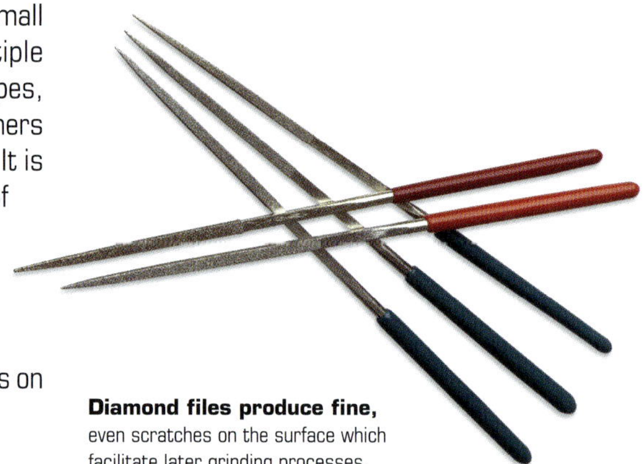

Diamond files produce fine, even scratches on the surface which facilitate later grinding processes.

To square a sheet into a right angle it is important to use a set square. After filing one of the sides put this at a right angle to the set square with the light behind it. After checking that the points of the piece are against the set square, file the piece again on these points. Repeat this process on all sides of the piece until a perfect right angle is achieved.

Looking after and cleaning files

It is important to keep files in good condition. It is advisable to keep them separate from the rest of the jewelry-making tools to avoid them wearing away when they rub together. It is a good idea to have specific files for working with each metal. Soft metals, such as copper, can clog the files easily. Remnants of lead can damage the piece with holes or taint the metal when it is annealed again. When filing pieces of gold, it is very important that the files are in perfect condition and do not have remnants of other metals.

To clean them, it is advisable to use a special comb or to wash them with petrol; however, oil and excess heat should be avoided.

Beveling

Beveling and bending are processes that are often used in jewelry making. Many objects can be made, rings shaped, and settings made with pliers and small round files with different surfaces.

1/ This bracelet is made from a 1 mm sheet of silver onto which bevels have been made with differently sized openings. To do this, different files with square and triangular surfaces have been used.

2/ After annealing the sheet, bend the metal with parallel pliers until the desired angle is acquired.

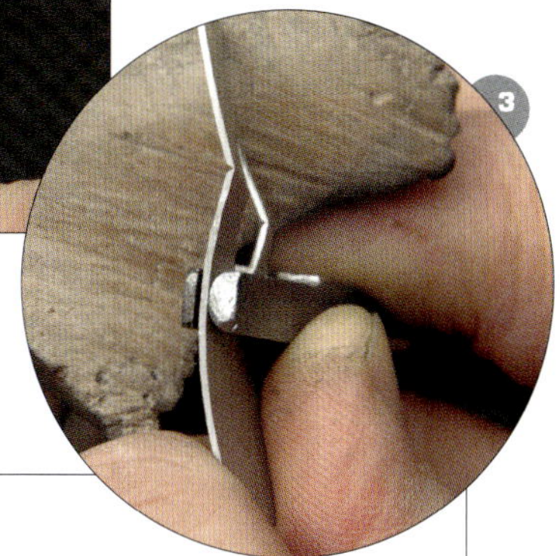

3/ With pliers, curve each side of the metal, adjusting the bracelet round.

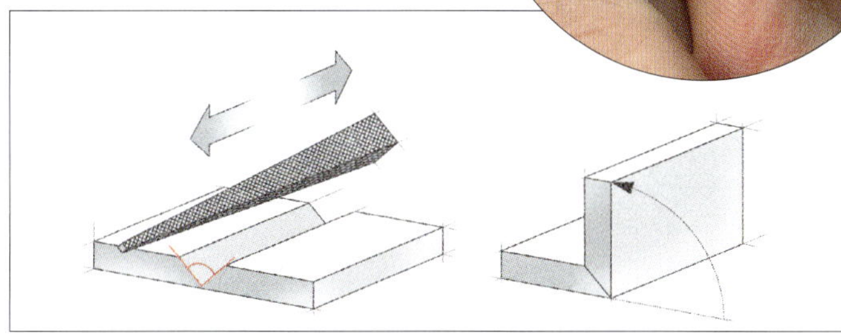

To make a 90° angle on the side, you need to cut a triangular notch into the metal; this will allow the wire to be bent at the right angle.

4/ Solder each bevel to make the bracelet stronger and stop it from breaking at one of the holes when it is being handled.

When the bracelet is completed, the finishing is done with a thick diamond file.

Sanding

The metal is generally sanded after the surface is filed in order to reduce the scratching left by the file or any other tool. It is essential to do the sanding well before starting the cleaning of the piece.

Emery paper has to be used in a continuous and consecutive fashion, always with the rough side on the surface. When the mark left by the file is quite apparent, begin with an aggressive paper, between 150 and 180. Follow this with a second paper with a number close to 400, a third paper of around 650, and, lastly, use an extra-fine paper of 1200.

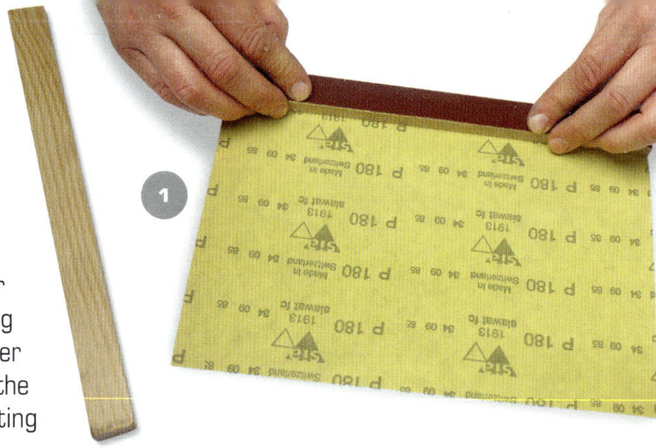

Emery sticks

One of the most useful tools that can be made very cheaply is an emery stick. They are made using pieces of emery paper, of different grades, stuck onto various pieces of wood. This very simple tool allows for better control and precision for sanding work, as well as getting the most from the paper.

1/ To prepare emery sticks, cut various pieces of wood of different sizes, always of the length of the emery paper to be used. Next, fold the paper around the piece of wood and secure with your fingers.

2/ With the ends of some scissors, mark each of the folds and cut the paper to the exact size.

3/ Adhere the paper onto the wood with wood glue.

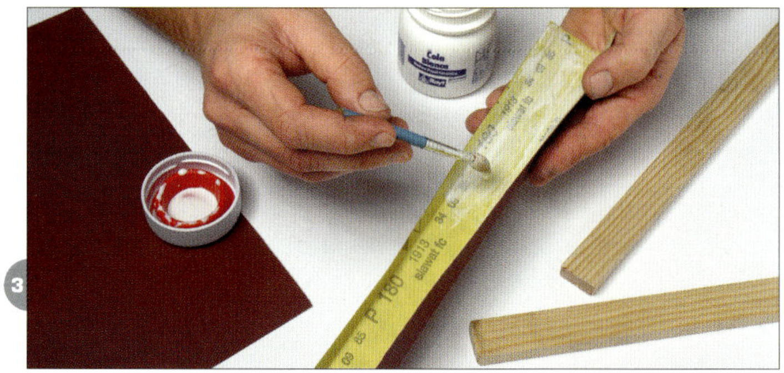

4/ Press down with your fingers, ensuring that the glue does not enter into contact with the surface of the emery paper, and leave it until it is completely dry.

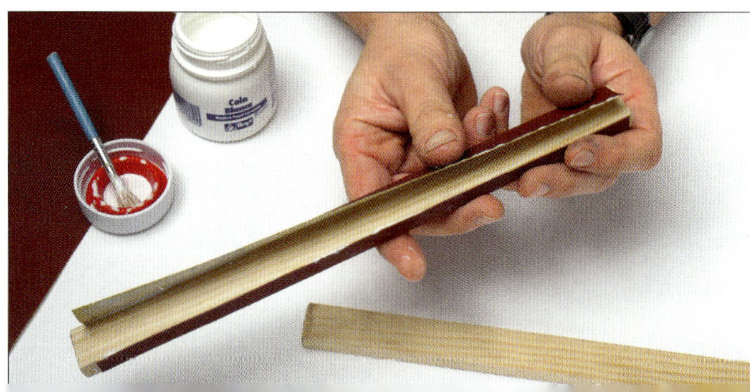

Red corundum emery paper is suitable for achieving a good finish on metal, but to obtain the best sanding, it is important to use the emery paper in a continuous order, from coarse to very fine grade. In the picture, there are various sheets of emery paper with different grades.

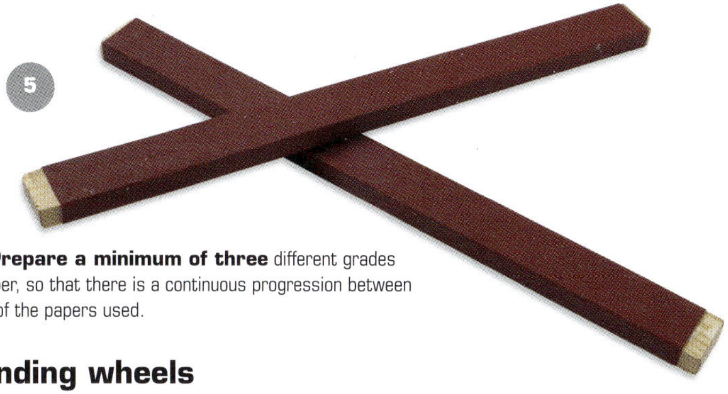

5/ Prepare a minimum of three different grades of paper, so that there is a continuous progression between each of the papers used.

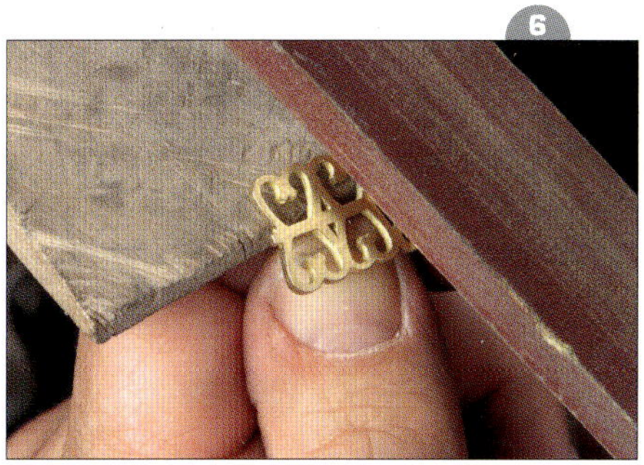

6/ With the sand paper stuck onto the piece of wood flat surfaces are sanded by criss-crossing the surface to avoid grooves. The finished surface needs to be smooth and even.

Sanding wheels

An electric sanding machine can also be used with sanding wheels. They are put together very simply and are practical and effective for sanding the inside of rings and small pieces that are difficult to reach. It is important to use them correctly, so as not to leave marks on the sanded surfaces. To put them together, just use strips of emery paper 1 cm wide and tie them to the end of a mandrel with steel soldering wire.

1/ The sanding wheels are prepared by various strips of emery paper of different grades being fixed to them.

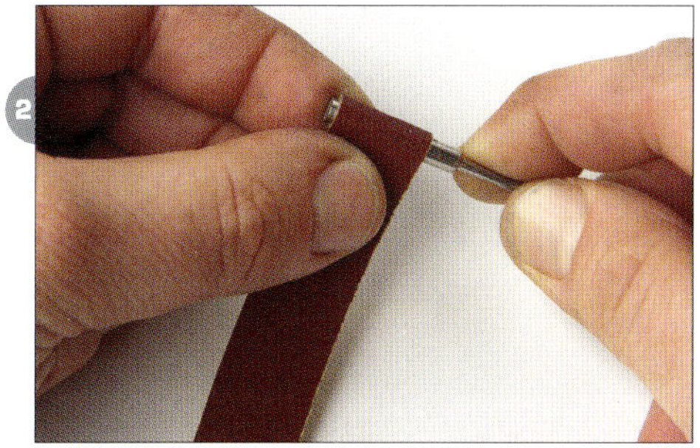

2/ Wrap the paper around the inside of the wheel and tie with steel wire at one end.

3/ These tools are useful for sanding the inside of rings or other shapes, but not for sanding flat sheets as they often leave deep grooves.

Sanding machine

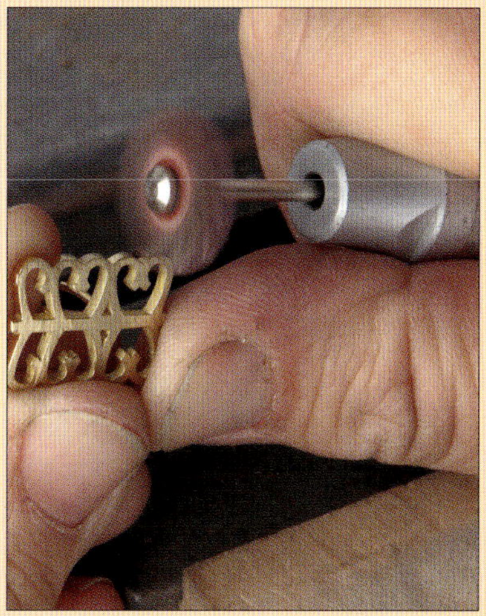

This is often used in finishing work and casting sanding as it gives a good progressive finish on smooth surfaces or the inside of rings and bracelets. It is advisable to wear protective gloves and eyewear when using it to avoid metal particles coming into contact with the skin and eyes.

It is also advisable to use a suitable space that allows for the recovery of the metal particles that fly out due to the speed of the sanding machine.

Working with wire and plates

Once the metal is melted and placed inside an ingot mold, in the shape of an ingot or a rail, one of the three basic elements for making pieces of jewelry and gold and silver work can be obtained: a sheet, a wire, or a tube.

These elements can be acquired from a specialist supplier, but it is necessary to know how to make them, especially when working with gold. It helps to keep costs down as remnants from the workbench can be recovered, and different and innovative shapes can be obtained.

To obtain sheets or wire of different shapes, start with metal rails cast in an ingot mold. These shapes facilitate later flattening or drawing of the metal.

It is practical to buy sheets of laminated silver of the desired thickness. Sheets or wires that have been previously annealed or strengthened sheets can be obtained. The sheets are protected by a very flat and almost polished sheet of plastic.

Inés Sobreira. Pins made from 18k gold with filigree technique from gold wire.

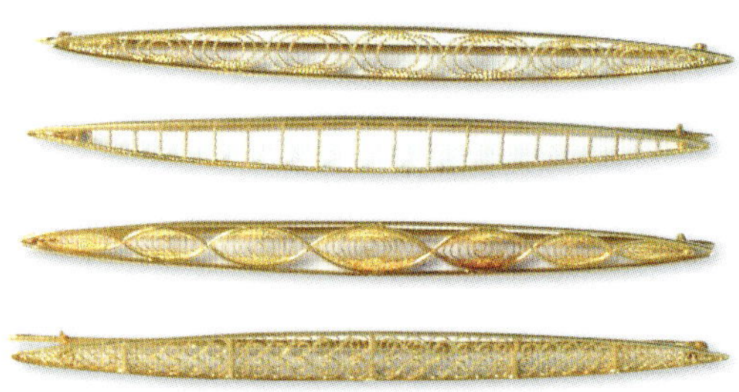

Ulla and Martín Kaufmann. Necklace of forged yellow gold made from a sheet of pure gold.

Rolling sheets of metal

Before beginning to make sheets of gold or silver, it is advisable to compress the ingot correctly, hitting it with a heavy hammer on all sides.

This process is vital for platinum. Afterwards, the ingot is rolled in the rolling mill to obtain the desired reduction. Closing the upper mechanism of the press reduces the separation between the steel cylinders and, therefore, the metal becomes compressed and the size of the plate is reduced. This process requires continuous annealing. As a general rule, annealing should be done when the plate has reached a size of approximately half its original thickness.

The rolling mill is an important tool in any rolling process. There are small, mixed use presses, with which it is possible to roll plates and wire with the same tool. It can be fixed onto a strong table and is not too costly.

1/ It is advisable to compress the metal ingot with a heavy hammer before rolling. Hit it all over, especially on the corners.

2/ Turning the upper screw on the rolling mill gradually reduces the separation between the two cylinders of the mill and reduces the size of the ingot until it is turned into a sheet of a particular thickness.

3/ Continue rolling in the mill until the desired thickness is obtained. The direction that the sheet is put into the rolling mill should on no account be changed without the sheet having been annealed as the metal will break when it is returned to the laminator again.

4/ When the sheet is approximately half the size of the ingot, it needs to be annealed. Once it has been stripped and it is dry it can be laminated

Drawing wire

The same process of reducing and compressing is also used for cast rails; for this, a specific rolling mill is used which reduces the size of the rail to the desired size. Once this has been achieved, file one of the ends into a point and begin the drawing process on the drawing bench until a particular shape of wire is achieved. Wires, like sheets, must be annealed when they reach a size which is approximately half the size of the original.

1/ Various cast silver rails ready to be drawn into silver wire.

2/ Reduce the wire by gradually changing the channel on the wire roller. Start with the largest slot and continue by interchanging the sides of the wire round on the wheel to avoid the appearance of scales on the wire.

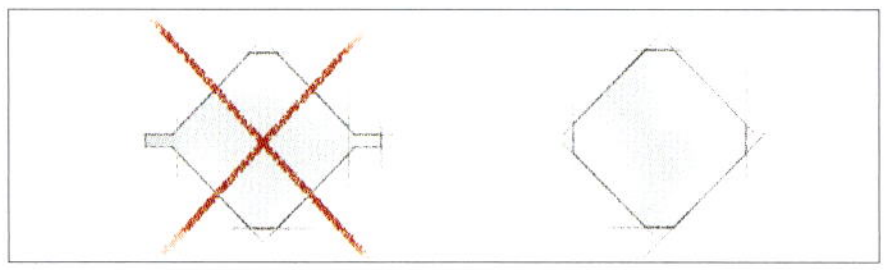

When using the wire roller, avoid the appearance of barbs on the ends of the rail due to too much pressure. If this happens they can be removed with a heavy file before continuing with the laminating.

3/ Continue with the reduction of the same wire until the desired result is achieved. Anneal the wire when it reaches half of its initial thickness; then strip it and rinse it in water before continuing the rolling.

4/ Once the rail is finished, file the point of the wire with a thick file so that it can fit through the hole of the drawing die.

5/ After annealing, choose a shape for the wire and pass the point of the wire through the hole whose size best corresponds to the size of the wire.

6/ On the drawing machine, begin to stretch the wire by its end. Gradually reducing the size of the holes will also reduce the size of the wire. Always following the order on the drawing die.

Tubes

Although it is possible to buy tubes of all sizes and without solder, it is necessary to know how to make a soldered tube as it is a shape that is often used in jewelry making. It is used for making clasps and settings for mounting stones, or for a variety of decorative elements. They can be made in all different kinds of shapes (round, square, oval, etc.), according to the die used.

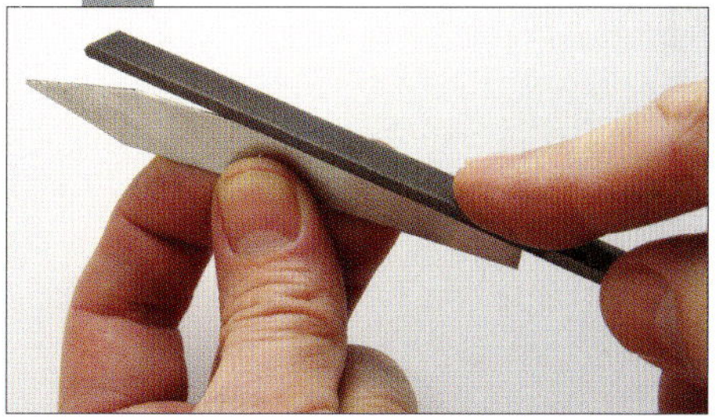

1/ To make a tube, begin by cutting a straight strip of metal of the desired thickness; then cut one of the ends in a V-shape. File the edges of the sheet to make the strip straight and to ensure that the soldering is correct.

2/ Using a rounded die with furrows and a correspondnig steel bar, put the sheet into the die and hit the steel bar with the plastic mallet until it fits the shape of the half tile.

3/ It is also possible to make a tube by directly tapping the inner part of the metal with the flat part of a jeweler's hammer. This also gradually reduces the size of the shape in the rounded die with furrows.

4/ This process is done gradually, using smaller and smaller furrows and bars of metal. The line of solder has to be perfectly aligned.

5/ To finish off the tube, use the flat side of the jeweler's hammer. Tap straight onto the outside of the metal until the tube is completely closed.

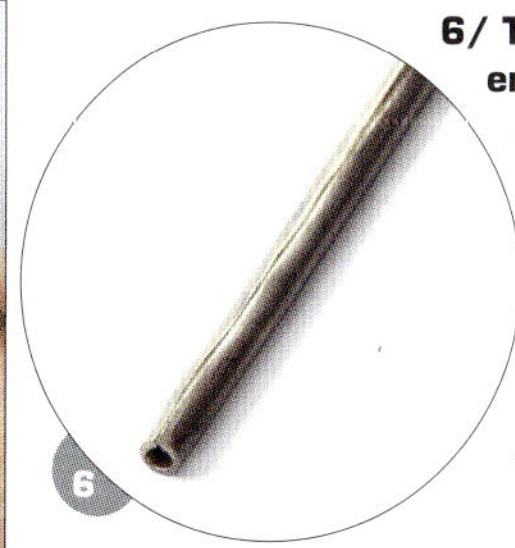

6/ The joining of the two ends of the tube must be perfect before being soldered. It is necessary to anneal the metal and go back to adjust the joint of the tube, as the tensions caused by the machining process can cause it to open up by a few tenths of a millimeter.

7/ Solder directly with soldering wire or by placing small cubes of solder, impregnated with liquid solder, onto the join, also impregnated with the same liquid. Now apply a reducing flame to encircle the join until the solder flows through the gaps along the join.

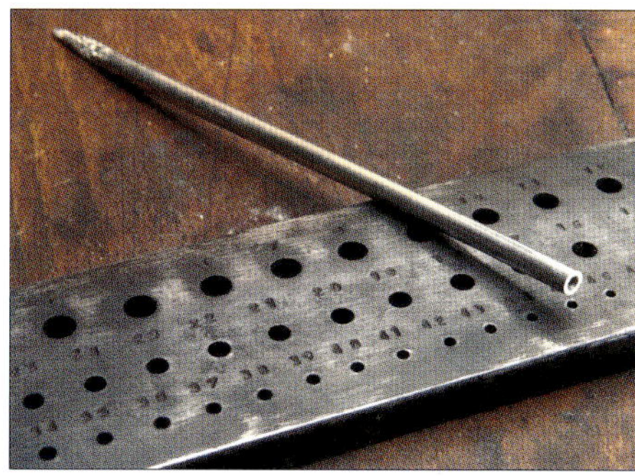

8/ Once stripped, remove the remains of solder which have stayed on the surface; then, draw it through the drawing die until the desired size tube is obtained.

Jump rings

Jump rings are made from different sized wires and used for all kinds of work. They can be used on their own to make chains, bracelets, or decorative rings, or as supports in a piece, for clasps or decorative elements. The process for making them consists of folding or bending wire of different sizes in a folding machine of a particular size.

1

1/ Small rings, also called jump rings, are made by rolling a wire, already annealed, around a steel shape called a folding machine. In this case, round silver rings are being made with round wire. It is very useful to use a small hand drill in the steel vise to get a large number of rings of equal size.

2/ To ensure that they have a well-rounded shape, use parallel pliers with a smooth interior to press down on the spiral at the same time as turning the handle of the hand drill. Once the wire spiral is bent it is annealed before the rings are cut.

2

Akiko Kurihara. ***Ring ring.*** **Rings made from lots of small gold and silver jump rings.**

3/ The spiral has to be cut lengthways; this can be done by hand, using a fret saw, or by machine with a cutter adapted to the hand piece of the flexible motor (as shown in the picture). This second option allows a great number of jump rings to be cut with precision.

3

4/ Close the spiral inside the support, mount the circular saw on the hand piece of the flexible motor, and put an aluminum support inside. Once it is fitted inside, just accelerate the motor at the same time as moving the hand piece lengthways.

5

5/ When the support is opened, the jump rings will be perfectly cut, but half open.

6/ To close them, use flat pliers.

6

Solder

Most metal objects are made from different metal elements joined by the support of a new alloy, generally made with the same metal as the piece being soldered, but with a lower melting point; this alloy is called solder. It can be bought from a specialist supplier or it can be made in the workshop; there are also other joints which do not require solder, such as joints made by arc welding or laser soldering.

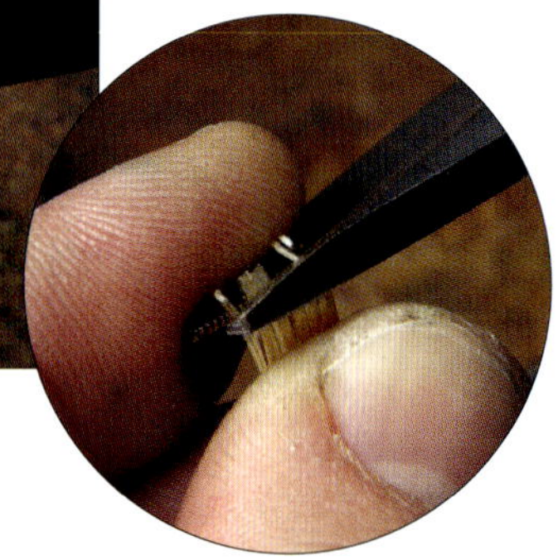

Make cuts lengthways and then cut across.

Once laminated to a thickness of 0.03 mm, clean thoroughly and cut into small pieces of approximately 1 mm before storing in a closed, labeled container.

Solder is found in specialist stores. There are solders with various melting points, ideal for soldering pieces with different joints. There is also solder in paste form with the flux included (this does not require liquid solder).

Soldering bricks are necessary for soldering and for annealing pieces on top of them. They must absorb the heat and not resist it. Soft bricks and brick made of charcoal are very useful.

Preparation

For gold solder, it is advisable to use prepared products especially made for this purpose. With these products, it is possible to obtain a good melting point, a good flow of solder once molten, correct malleability, and, most importantly, a good final color when the piece is polished.

For silver solder, it is necessary to melt this with an alloy containing between 60-70% copper and 30-40% zinc. It is not advisable directly to melt manufactured brass remnants, as their composition is unknown, and if it is not right, this will cause defects in the solder. To prepare solder, use a clean crucible suitable for this task. First cast the silver and then the rest of the metals which make up the final alloy, always in this order.

Each time a piece is soldered and stripped in acid, the solder suffers, as it contains metals, such as zinc or copper, that tend to disappear with oxidization and the stripping process, leaving the solder porous and prone to breaking.

Liquid solder

It is vital to use a good liquid solder based on borax, as this will avoid oxidization in the area being soldered, reduce the melting point, and help the solder to flow correctly over the whole joint. It is advisable to prepare liquid solder by mixing refined white borax with liquid yellow solder. Once the mixture is prepared, it is applied over the surface of the metal.

Sometimes, when annealing or before soldering, it is also advisable to protect the piece from oxidization with a good quality anti-oxidant made especially for this purpose. This will avoid the piece having direct contact with the flame and will therefore minimize the appearance of blue spots or burns on the silver.

For pieces that require soldering a number of times, and with the aim of avoiding the piece being damaged by the process, mixtures of graphite, red ocher, dry Indian ink or talcum powder are used.

Types of soldering

One of the most important tools in the workshop is the soldering iron. There are different models which use gas or other technology, and it is common to find soldering irons which run on butane or propane gas that combines with air pressure provided by a small compressor or pump. Other soldering irons that combine propane gas with oxygen pressure, oxhydric soldering irons, arc welding soldering irons, and laser soldering irons are also used.

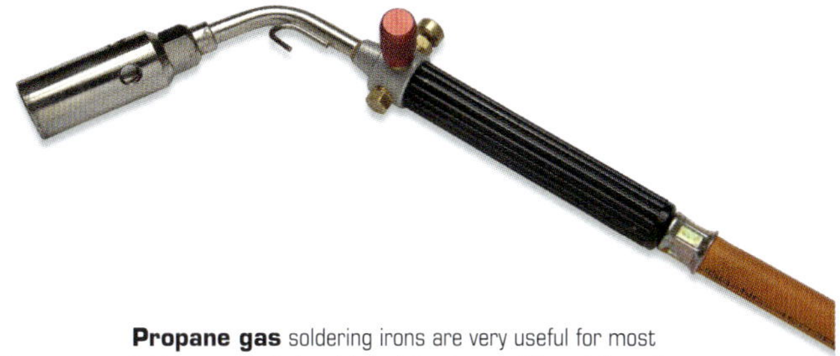

Propane gas soldering irons are very useful for most tabletop work. Being able to interchange different tips allows for the flame to be regulated easily and and permit it to be used on very specific areas of the piece.

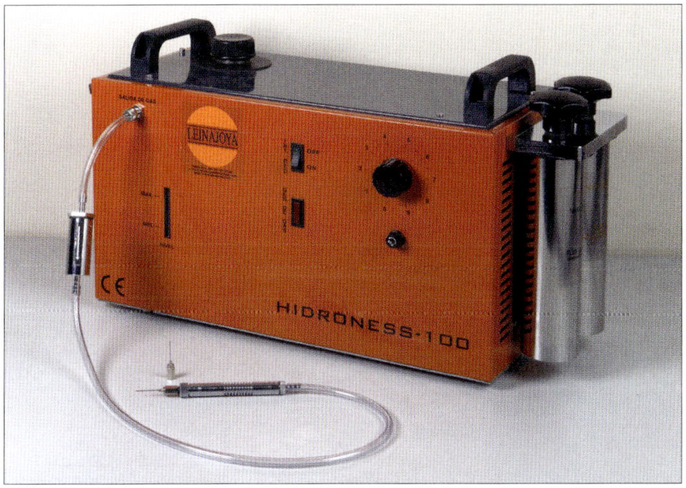

The oxhydric soldering iron is ideal for precision work, as it provides a precise high temperature flame that can be regulated. It is cheap and very safe.

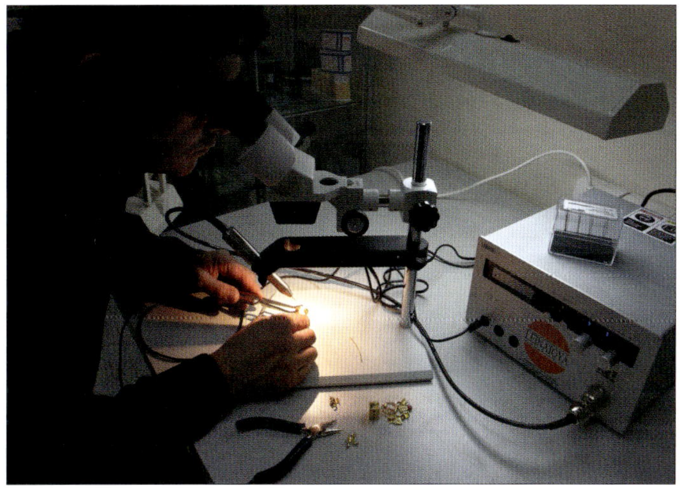

New arc welding and laser soldering equipment allow for the most inaccessible areas to be soldered and do not produce oxidization.

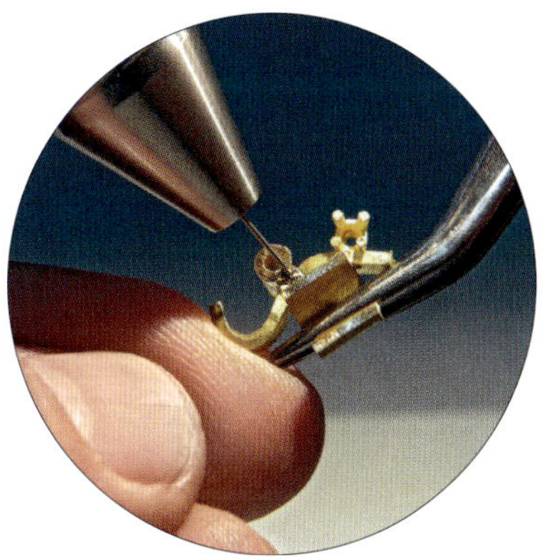

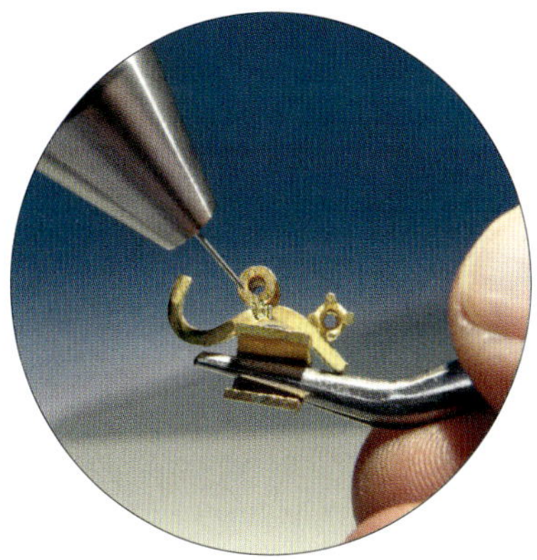

Arc welding and laser soldering supply new metal to the piece without it becoming hot. They are ideal for undertaking repairs without heating the piece.

Clasps and closures

Most pieces of jewelry require the making of specific structures with which bracelets, brooches, earrings, or necklaces are opened and closed. Making a clasp correctly is essential in jewelry, though often the clasps can be bought as ready-made findings, then soldered to the piece and adjusted afterwards.

In an artisan jewelry workshop, the jeweler often creates the structure of his or her own clasp, so that the piece of jewelry or object is unique. It is crucial that the clasp is aesthetically integrated into the work as a whole and that, due to its quality and beauty, makes up part of the piece itself or is very important to it.

Cold joints or rivets

When, due to the type of material used or the characteristics of the piece, it is not possible to solder or fix two or more sheets together, it becomes necessary to make a cold or mechanical join. This is a much-used method, either in the form of small screws or other types of rivets such as those shown here.

Riveting tubes

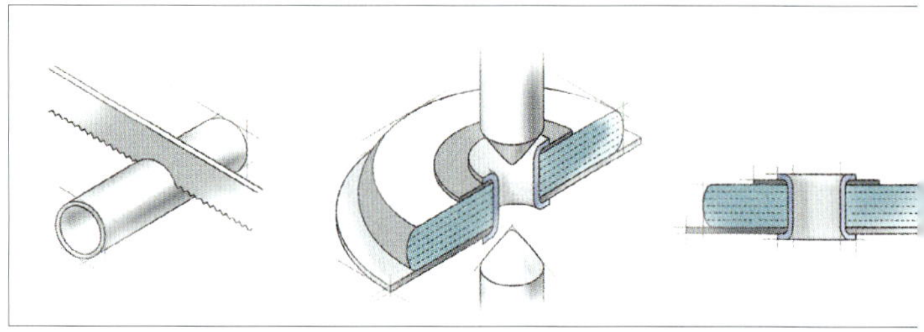

Tubes are useful for joining fragile and delicate materials (glass beads, stones, or plastic). The process consists of cutting a tube and, once it has been annealed, dilating the ends by turning the metal over the piece very carefully. This can be done directly on the piece or by placing a metal disc first, so that the dilated metal presses on the disc and not on the piece.

Riveting cloth and metal

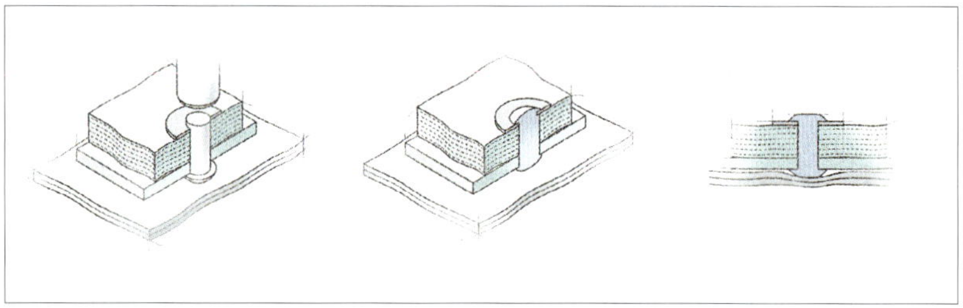

When one of the elements to be riveted is soft, make a calotte in one of the ends and forge the other end with the hammer on the die. A thick piece of paper or leather should be placed between the calotte and die so it does not become deformed.

Riveting metal to metal

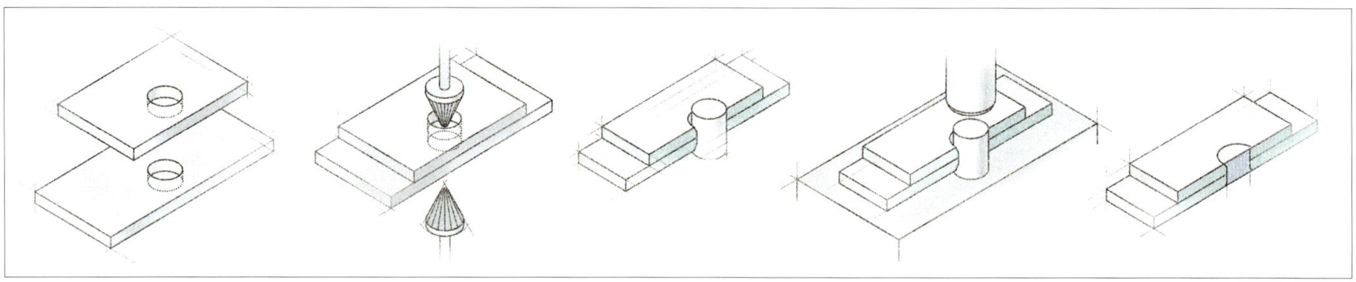

Make a hole in the same place in both sheets and pass an annealed wire through them that fits the inside of the holes perfectly. File the extra part so that the rivet overhangs by a few millimeters on each end; then forge on a steel die, pushing the nut outwards on the inside of the plates.

Earrings

In general, each type of earring requires a specific kind of clasp or closure, but the shape of the ear is also important, as is the weight of the earring or its ease of use. Making these clasps and closures requires working with metal that has already been tempered so that precise pressure is put onto another part of the structure and, therefore, allows it to be opened and closed.

A push-on back is ideal for light, stud earrings, the omega clasp is used in large heavier earrings, and wire backs are used for very light dangling earrings (usually with some type of structure or design hanging on the lower part).

Push-on back

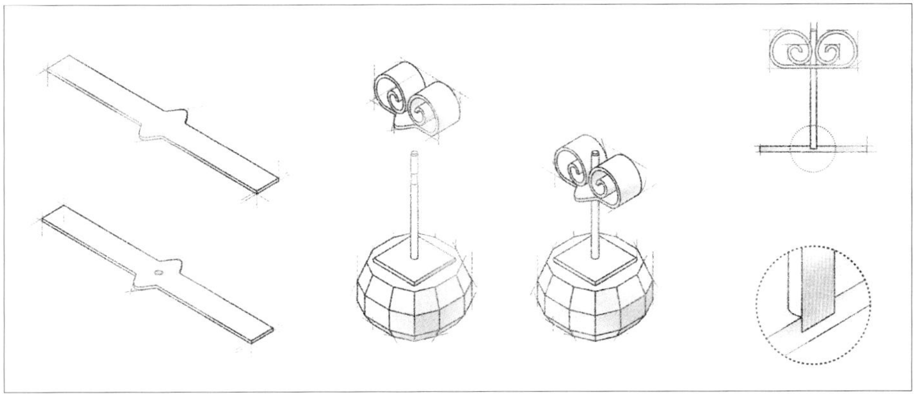

Take a sheet of tempered metal 0.02 and make a hole in the center; then turn the ends over with round-nose pliers.

The back works by the pressure put on the post by the tempered metal, joined to the main structure of the earring.

Omega clasp

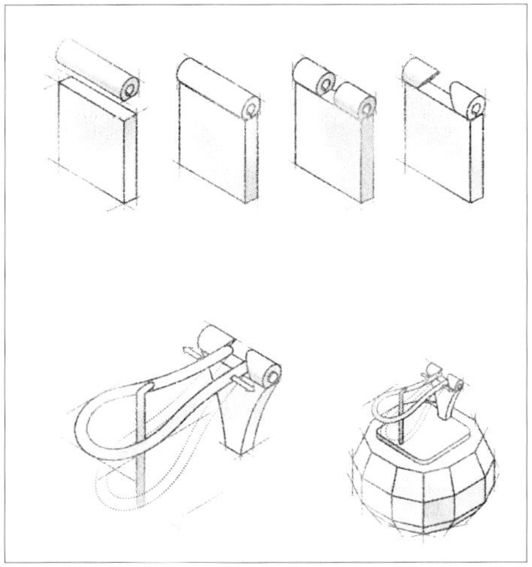

This clasp is ideal for flat wide earrings, and is easy to adjust and fit to different ear shapes. It works by the pressure exerted by a small structure in the Omega (Ω) shape on the back which acts as a support. This structure cannot be annealed. It must always be mounted and unmounted cold to avoid the tempering being lost.

Rubber backs

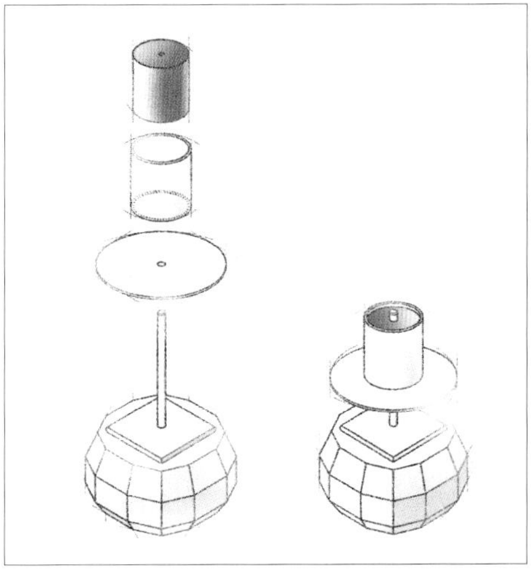

Insert a small piece of gasket, usually high-density rubber, fit it, and stick it to the inside of a metal tube that has already been soldered onto a flat disc. The closure works by the pressure put on the metal by the metal post. This is also used for making small pins.

Wire back

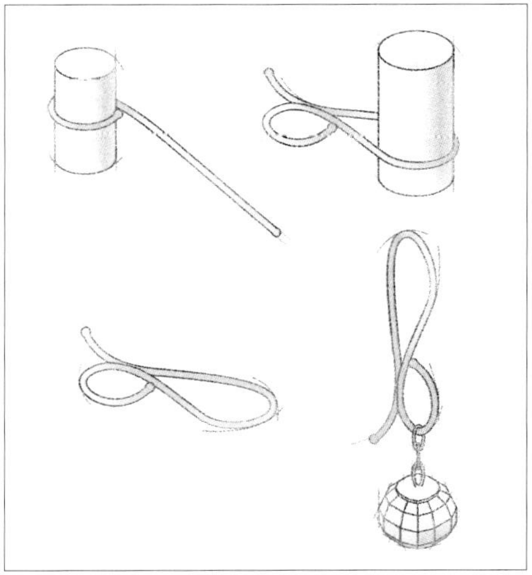

These earring backs, of which many different versions can be made, are used for light earrings with hanging parts that are also light (glass beads, pearls, or other decorations). They are made from tempered wire and are folded cold; sometimes, some areas have to be forged cold to improve the tempering of the wire.

Brooches

Although there are many varieties, the brooches shown here are those with the most common types of clasp.

Pins are better if they are made with dental steel. If they are made in gold or silver the wire needs to have a degree of tension or tempering, therefore a tempered wire should be used. For this, anneal the wire and draw it through three consecutive holes.

Bayonet clasp

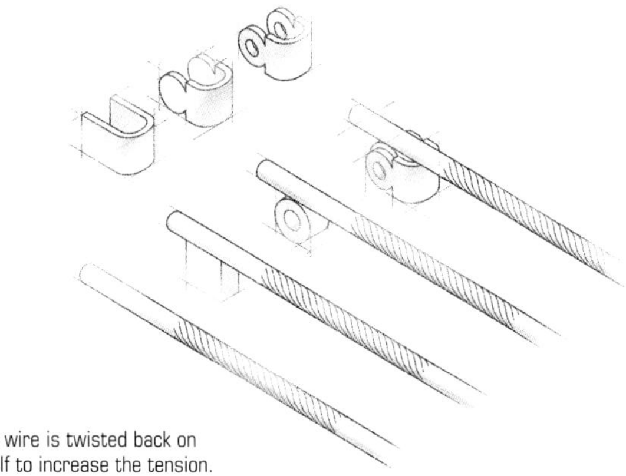

The wire is twisted back on itself to increase the tension.

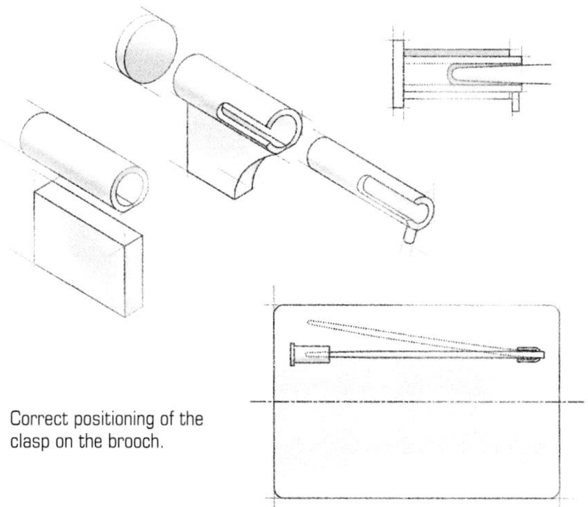

Correct positioning of the clasp on the brooch.

This is one of the most often used clasps for brooches. It has three separate parts: the support for the pin, the clasp or bayonet, and the pin, which will be riveted to the support. With just one pin, it is necessary to solder the clasp on the upper third of the brooch, as indicated in the drawing, to achieve good positioning on the body.

Double pin clasp

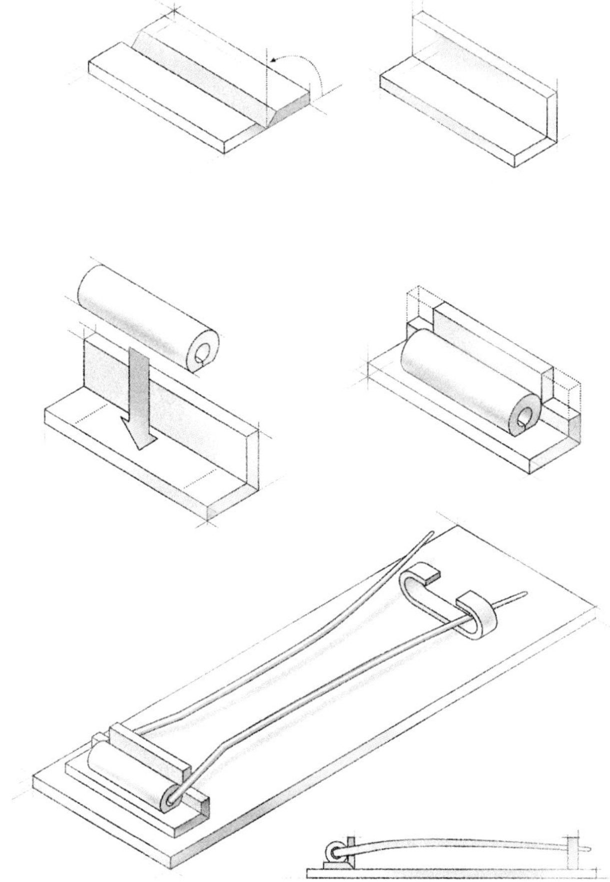

This is ideal for large, heavy brooches. As it has a double pin, the brooch fits perfectly against the garment and does not move around. The pin consists of a tempered wire passed through the tube of the clasp and then bent; sometimes dental steel can be used to make the double pin.

Necklaces and bracelets

The clasps shown here are structures that need to be reinterpreted so they fit with the characteristics of each piece and to the aesthetic tastes of each jeweler. In general, they can be used for necklaces, bracelets, and other structures that need to be temporarily joined. They work by the tension exerted by tempered metal on the other structures; therefore annealing of the areas that require a hard metal with tension should be avoided.

Wire clasp

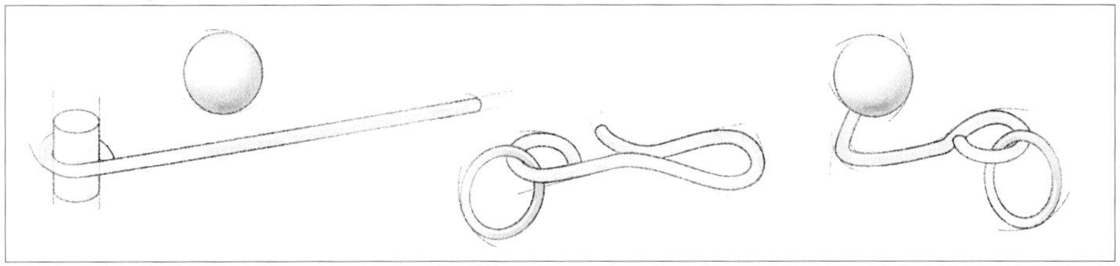

This type of clasp, ideal for bracelets or delicate necklaces, allows for many creative possibilities. It is made with different sizes of wire. To make it, a tempered wire is needed, which is then folded so it maintains the stiffness needed for it to work properly. Sometimes, it is necessary to use a hammer to forge some areas that need increased hardness. This increases the tension and improves the performance of the clasp.

Box clasp

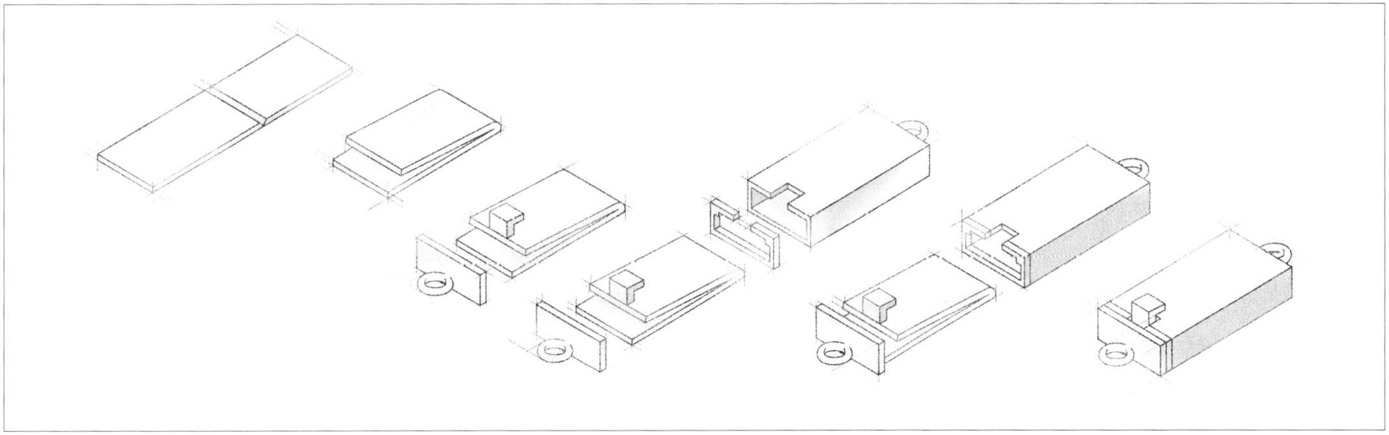

This is a classic clasp used for bracelets, bangles, and necklaces. It usually is fitted underneath or inside a link so that it cannot be seen from the outside. It works by the tension exerted by the tab when inserted inside a closed box. A variant of this is the tab clasp, ideal for bracelets or light bead necklaces.

Tab clasp

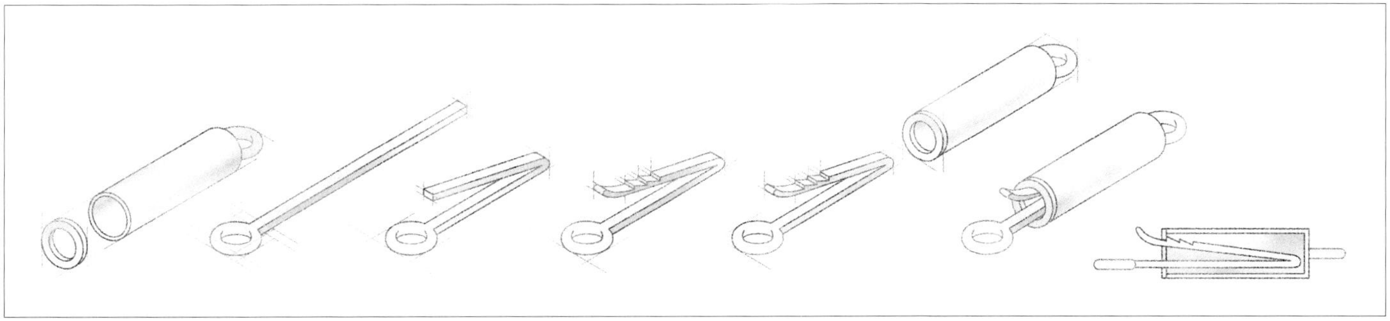

Ball clasp

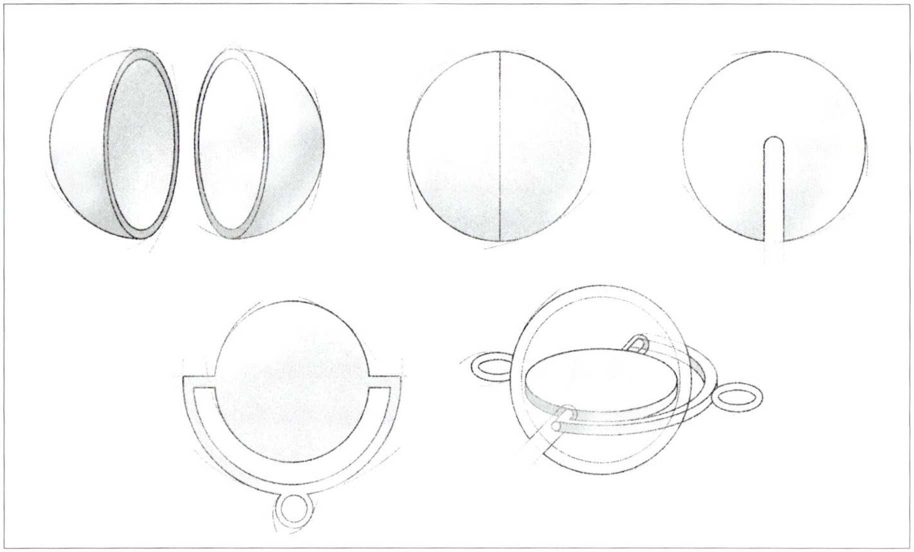

There are many variants of the ball-type clasp. It is formed by two soldered half spheres and a piece of thick metal plate which fits inside the sphere. It is ideal for bead necklaces of some importance and allows for the outside of the sphere to be decorated. The sphere is made first, then a cut of 1 mm is made in it. This is where the cut out shape, made from metal plate of the same thickness, is inserted from the other end of the necklace or bracelet.

Barrel clasp

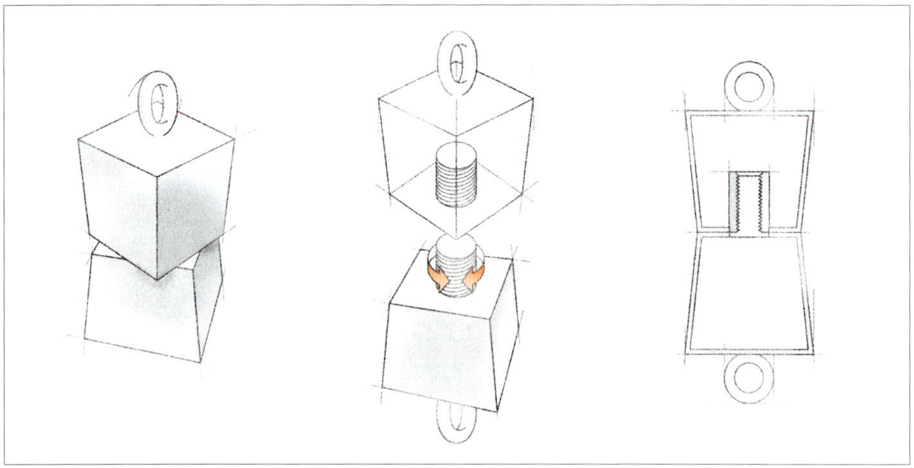

The barrel clasp consists of a central screw and an inner tube with an inner screw the same size as the central screw. This is then adapted to a clasp structure. This type of joint can be used not only with bracelets and necklaces, but also with any structure that needs to be opened.

To make the central screw and the inner screw of the silver tube, a set of male screws of the same metric size is needed, which can be found at any hardware suppliers.

Pearl necklace clasp

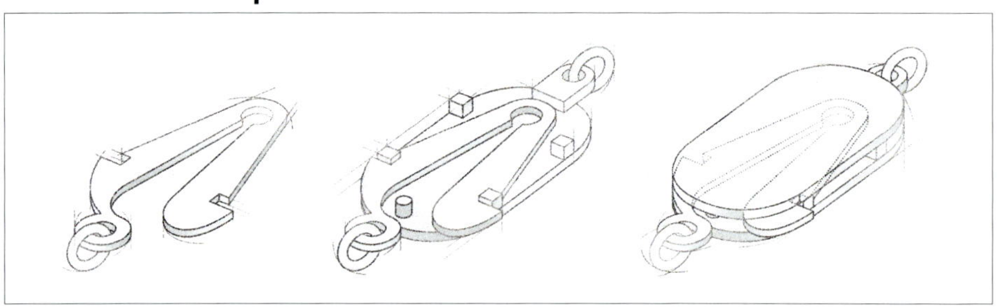

Traditionally, this is used for pearl necklaces or any other type of bead necklace. The advantage of this clasp is that, if it opens accidently, the necklace does not come completely undone, as it is caught by the design of the inner tab. It is important that the tab has a degree of tension; therefore, an unannealed plate, that will not be annealed later, is used for the cut out.

Hinge clasp with pin

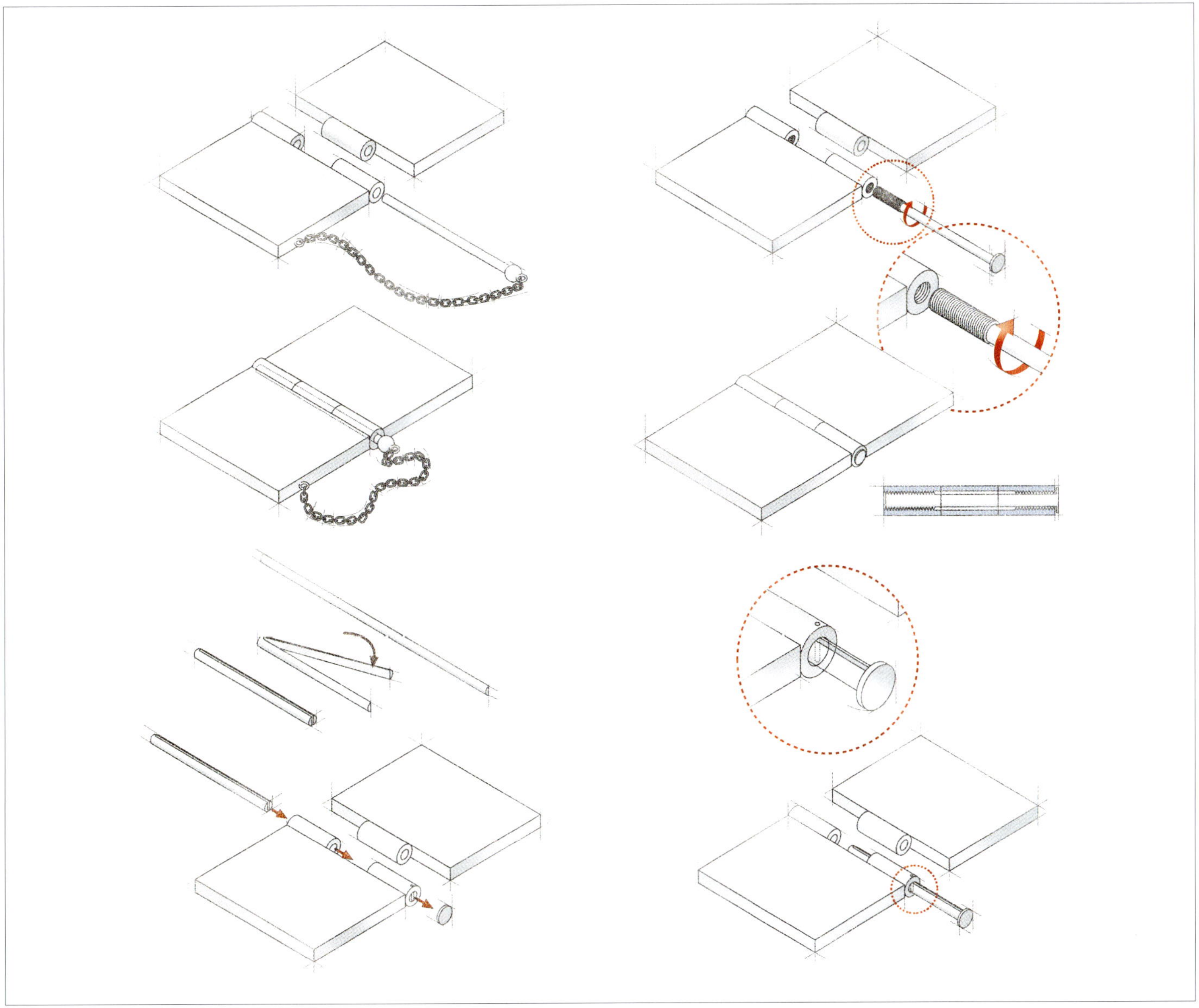

These clasps are generally used for wide bangles and arm cuffs and there are many variants, some of which are shown in the drawing. They have a double advantage: apart from perfectly integrating the clasp mechanism into the structure of the piece, the clasp itself also works as hinge, making it suitable for use with hinged bracelets. It has a pin that, when removed, frees the adjoining part, allowing it to be opened and closed.

"Solitaire" ring

In this section, the making a very simple silver ring is explained, using rectangular silver wire and a sheet of silver that has been cut and soldered using an oxhydric soldering iron. It will show a basic process, using a round ring adjusted to fit the size of a particular finger.

Due to their importance, the filing and sanding processes are highlighted, particularly the final finish of the ring, which shows the oxidization process of the silver and also the diamond sanding process that is the final finish of the piece.

1/ Take the finger measurement with a numbered ring measurer. This can give a direct indication of the diameter and its linear development. For our purposes we need to add 40 mm to the diameter measurement, plus twice the thickness of the wire being used. This will determine the initial development of the silver wire and the exact length.

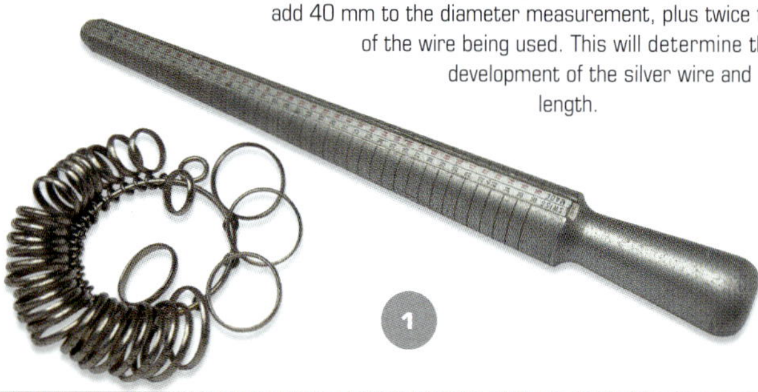

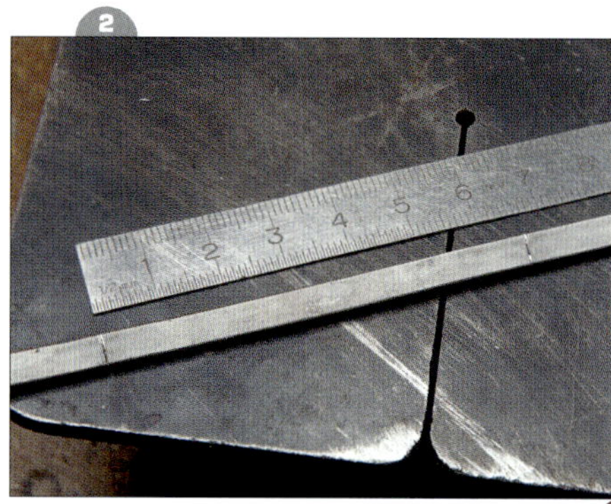

2/ On this occasion, the measurement was 19 and the thickness of the wire, 3. The calculation was:
19 + 40 + 6 = 65 mm.
Once the length of ring has been determined, transfer this measurement to the wire using two marks made with a punch or saw.

3/ Once the line of the ring has been marked, bend it, forcing it over the round ring plate by tapping it with a nylon mallet. This process is easier and more precise if a small tool specifically designed for bending shapes is used, especially when thick wire needs to be bent without marking the surface of the metal.

4/ Bend the ring over until the two marks meet, and cut with a fretsaw.

5/ Anneal and tap the plate again to get a perfectly fitting joint for the ring. Then, press by hand or with pliers, and saw the joint again. This process gives a perfect fit and secures the solder.

6/ Now, place a small piece of solder on the joint and apply heat. Let it cool, then strip to remove the surface oxide.

7/ The ring must be perfectly round. To achieve this, use the round steel plate and tap with a nylon mallet. This process requires great care to avoid the ring taking on a conical shape.

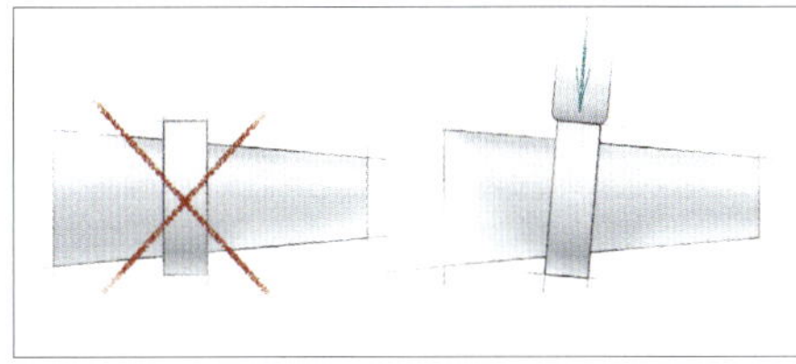

8/ Give the ring taps on alternate sides, changing the angle on the plate on both sides so as not to leave it in a tapered shape. Never tap it by forcing down the end of the plate; the ring must always be hit with a flat tap to keep its straight tubular shape.

9/ With a medium grain flat file, file the two sides of the ring, then use a semi-circular file to file the inside. In the same manner, file the upper part, removing any irregularities and evening out the thickness of the ring all around.

10/ The sanding process is vital. All the surfaces must be gradually sanded, in the same way as they were filed previously. In this case, various red corundum emery papers have been used: starting with 180, 450, and 600 grades, and working down to 1200 paper.

11/ Sand the inside of the ring well by fixing various grades of sand papers on a sanding wheel with a rotary tool.

12/ To make this eye-catching *solitaire* ring, a figure has been cut out of 1.3 mm silver plate. On the foot, a small, 1 mm, extra piece has been left to fit it to the ring. With a millimeter drill bit, make a small hole in the central part of the ring where the figure can be inserted and soldered.

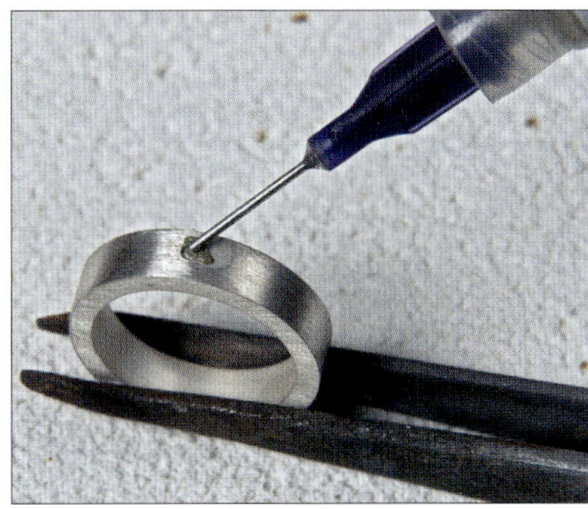

13/ Apply solder paste to the inside of the hole and fill it with heat from the oxhydric soldering iron. This solder paste includes flux in its mix, meaning that the only preparation needed is to ensure that the parts to be soldered are clean and free of oxide.

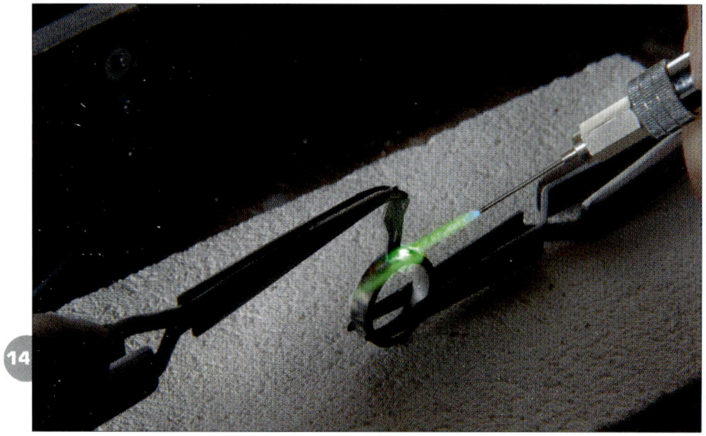

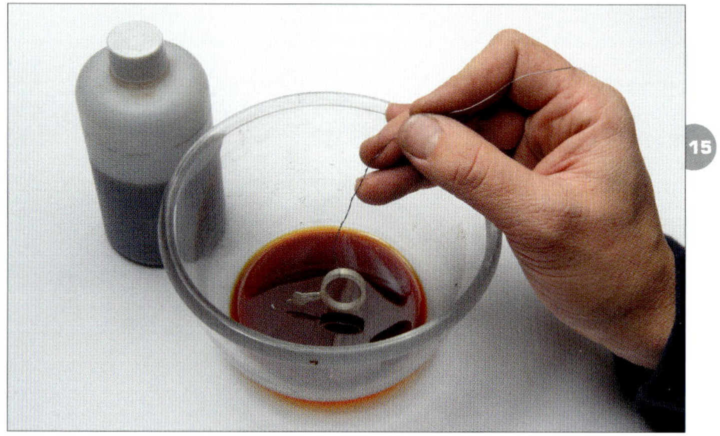

14/ The oxhydric flame only heats the soldering area, without unnecessarily oxidizing the metal, which allows for fast precision soldering. Insert the figure.

15/ After stripping and cleaning the piece thoroughly, prepare silver oxide in a glass container and hang the piece from a steel wire to avoid contact between the sulfur and your fingers.

16/ Submerge the piece in silver oxide for a few seconds until the silver is completely oxidized. To fix this oxide without creating marks on the surface, boil some water and hold the piece in the steam.

17/ Lastly, scratch one of the surfaces of the ring with diamond sandpaper. Metal varnish needs to be applied all over the surface in order to protect it and strengthen the black color produced by the silver oxide.

Carles Codina. ***Solitaire.*** **Oxidized silver ring with one side scratched with diamond sandpaper.**

Pendant with clasp

This section shows how to make a gold pendant with glass beads that hangs from a fine steel wire twisted to form a necklace. The process includes explanations of how to make a setting and how to forge a wire in order to make a particular part of the metal stronger.

The most interesting aspect of this section is the integration of the clasp into the pendant. It is, in this case, an idea for a pendant clasp that can be interpreted in different ways; the shape of the forging just needs to be adapted to the various shapes and sizes of the necklaces being made.

1/ To make the ends of the cable that support the pendant, prepare a small tube of silver, approximately 1.5 mm in diameter on the outside, with an inner hole of 0.05 mm. Separately, cast two pieces of silver over a small hole made in the charcoal brick. The aim is to make two irregular balls to which small pieces of the tube will be soldered.

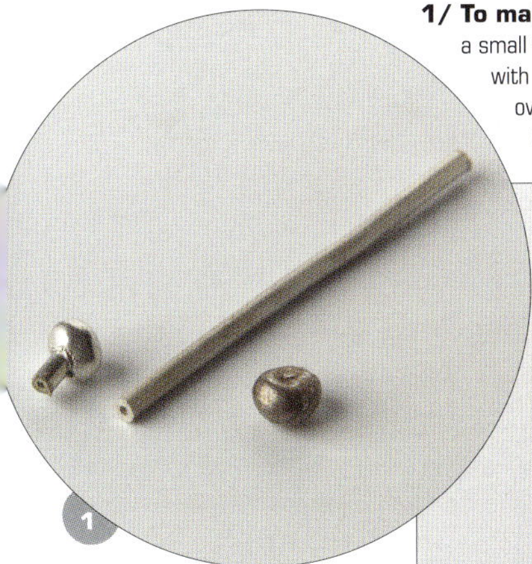

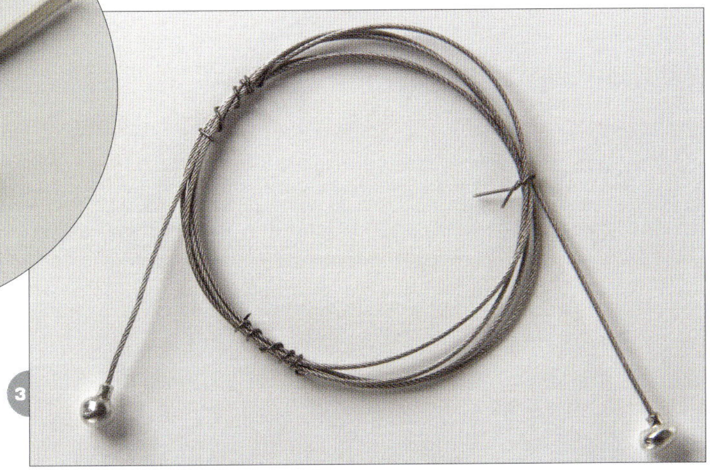

2/ Insert an end of the 0.05 mm steel cable into the inside of the tube and press it firmly using round-nose pliers to fix the cable at the end. The cable can also be fixed by applying a small drop of cyanoacrylate glue on the end.

3/ Cut the required amount of cable then add the tube and ball at the other end.

5/ Finish by closing the tube in the die, solder it, and draw it through the drawing die until a tube of around 5 mm in diameter has been obtained.

6/ With the saw, cut a piece of this tube about 2 cm, then sand it and even up the ends.

4/ On a die with furrows press a 0.05 mm plate to make a gold tube.

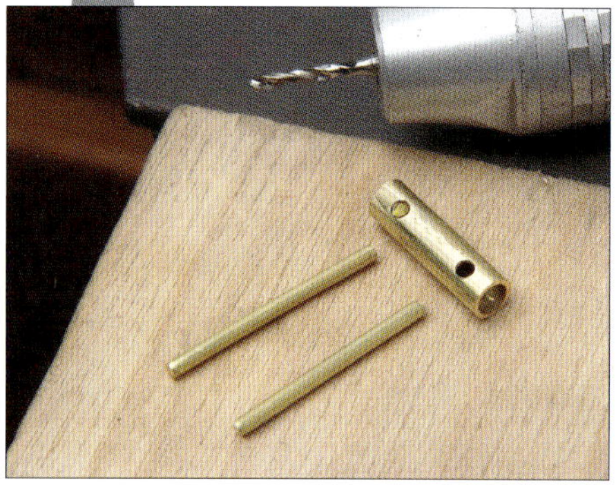

7/ Prepare two pieces of 1.3 mm round wire and make holes in the tube as shown in the photo.

8/ Solder the two wires to the inside of the tube and remove the surplus from inside with a spherical mill cutter.

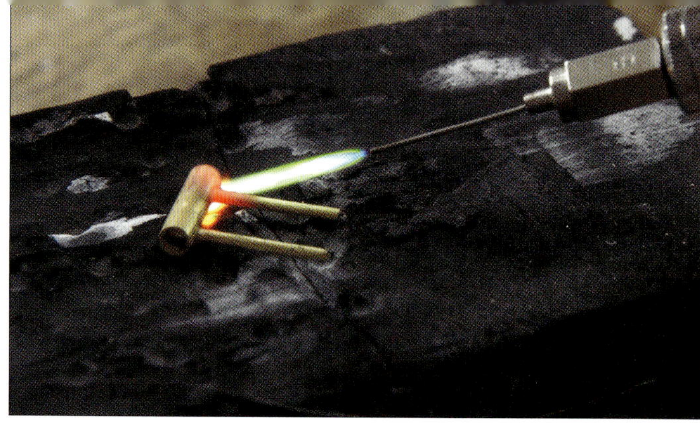

9/ On a die, forge the ends of the two round wires to make a spade shape. This forging widens out the wire at the end and gives it hardness or tempering.

10/ File the wires to even out the metal. Then sand and polish both ends.

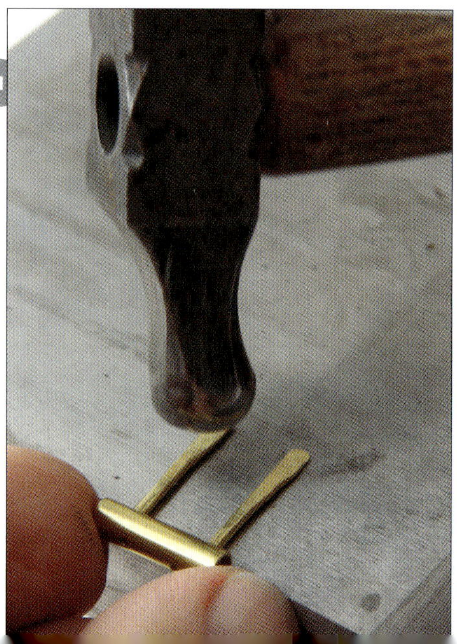

11/ With a well-polished ball-peen hammer, forge all of the spades again to obtain a uniform "martelé" effect on the surface.

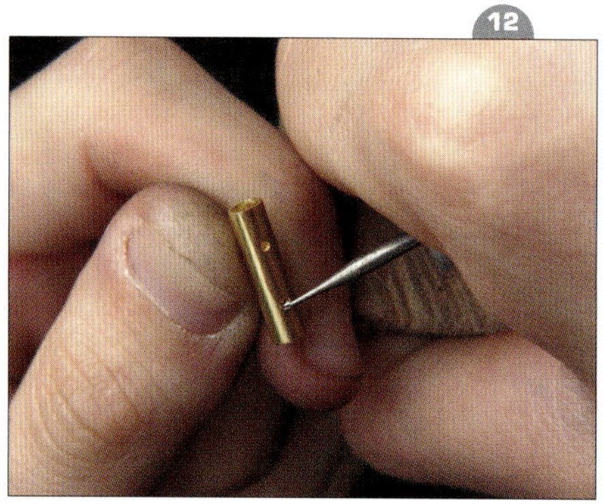

12/ With the help of a 0.04 mm ball cutter, make holes through the gold tube.

13/ Separately, use a 1 mm thick rectangular wire, beveled into an L-shape, to make a setting for a small tourmaline. See pages 51-52.

14

14/ Once this structure is finished, solder the tube, and then, with the help of round-nose pliers, turn the forged spade shape over the gold tube.

15/ Using 0.05 mm wire, make a small molten ball at the end. This will support the glass beads.

15

16

16/ Select various glass beads, for their shape and color, and fix the tourmaline in its place. Lastly, oxidize the silver ends of the steel cable and finish the gold structure.

17

17/ Now thread the glass beads onto the gold wire and, with round-nose pliers, bend the ends of the wires to secure the beads.

18

18/ The finished pendant. There can be many variations depending on the type of beads or other chosen elements. CodinaOrfebres.

Ring with tourmaline

For this gold ring, a yellow tourmaline of extraordinary purity has been chosen. To make the piece of jewelry, a piece of square wire is needed and a setting made in flat wire, which will be soldered onto a round, previously textured disc. The piece is made of two very simple elements, wire and cut gold plate, but it introduces some basic construction processes often used in jewelry: bending a shape with pliers, soldering gold, filing and sanding, as well as mounting a gemstone, and texturing metal. To finish, it shows the final polishing of the piece, an essential process for finishing any piece of jewelry, which gives the ring the desired touch of splendor.

1

1/ First make 1.8 mm thick, previously annealed and stripped, square gold wire.

2/ With your fingers or with the help of parallel pliers, bend the wire around a round steel plate and pull firmly at the ends.

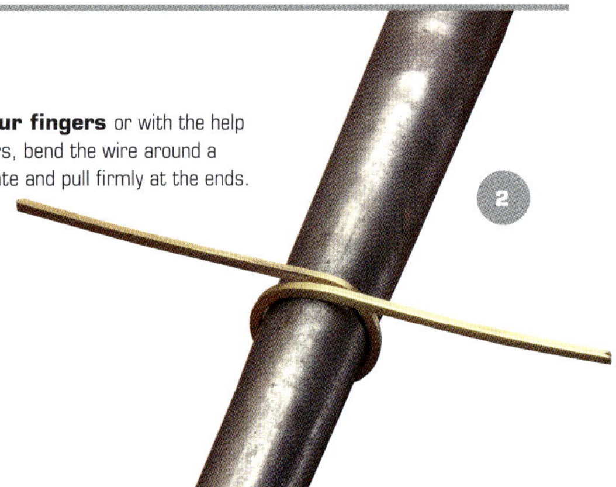

2

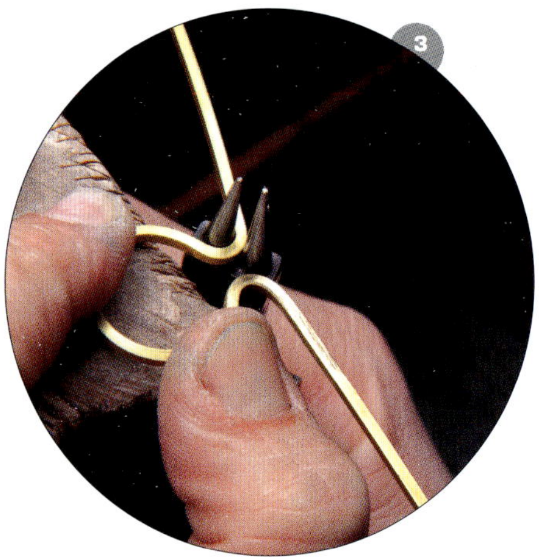

3

3/ Round-nose pliers allow an outer loop in the square wire to be made. Soldering of the ring will be done at this point, which at the same time will function as a base for the circular bowl that will hold the setting for the gemstone.

4

4/ With flat, round-nose pliers, it is easier to adjust the upper part of the ring and turn the wire around without marking it.

5

5/ Once the side of the wire has been flattened with a nylon mallet on a steel die, file and sand the whole surface of the ring. A gradual reduction of three grades of emery paper must be used with a final sanding with a 1200 grade paper.

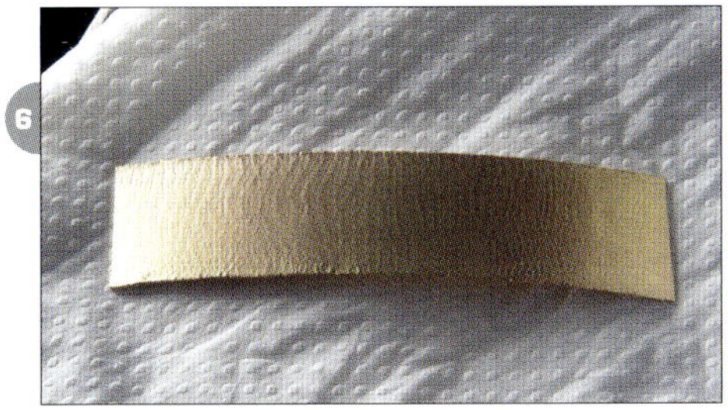

6/ For the bowl prepare a 0.07 thick, previously annealed, gold sheet, then roll in the rolling mill together with textured kitchen towel to obtain a subtle surface texture.

7/ Insert the sheet into the disc cutter and cut a shape of approximately 2 cm.

8/ To slightly curve the disc, put it in a wide press like the one in the picture.

9/ To avoid damaging the textured surface of the gold, put a little of the same kitchen towel onto this side of the metal. By hand, and avoiding any type of tapping, press the gold disc onto the inside surface of the press with an outward, rounded movement.

10/ The disc should be slightly sloped and free from all marks.

11/ To make the setting for the tourmaline, take a rectangular wire or a 1 mm thick by 6 mm high plate. Flatten it in the die, and make a 90° bevel with a triangular file. After annealing the metal, bend it using flat pliers and solder the join.

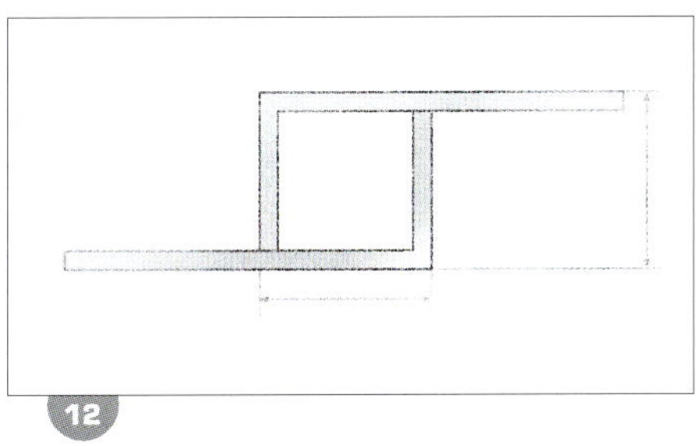

12/ To make a square or rectangular shape for the setting, make two L-shaped pieces that are soldered together, and then cut the surplus ends; in this way, the right shape is obtained for the size of the gemstone.

13/ The setting for the stone is formed from the two L-shapes in the form of a rectangle; on this occasion, a yellow tourmaline of exceptional quality has been chosen. The setting has been made to the exact measurements of the stone.

13

14

14/ Using small, flat and triangular files, the metal of the setting has been cut by filing the upper and lower parts.

15

15/ Once the setting is finished, it is soldered into the center of the bowl.

16/ When the ring and the bowl, with its soldered setting, are finished, the two structures are soldered. Two small pieces of gold, medium-grade solder are placed on the join and heat is applied with the soldering iron.

16

17

17/ The structure of the ring after being sanded with fine emery, once the soldering is finished.

18/ Now the process of setting the tourmaline starts. With a rotary tool using a ball or spherical cutter, make a slot inside each side of the setting onto which the gemstone will fit.

19/ Diagram of the different phases of setting a gemstone.

20/ Once the tourmaline is placed in its setting, file off a little of the excess metal, and, with a press or pneumatic hammer, tap the exterior metal, knocking it onto the stone.

21/ File and sand the metal on the outside edges of the setting.

22/ Remove the excess metal remaining on the gemstone by using a file or flat burin. Polish or lightly burnish the metal in contact with the stone and it will be ready to polish.

23/ Before polishing, it is advisable to use a soft rubber brush to obtain an even finer finish.

24/ To polish, first apply a strong abrasive paste to completely eliminate the scratches left over from the sanding. Choose a green paste and apply it to a felt disc.

25/ For this side, first polish the flat sides of the ring. Always polish the piece on the inner part of the disc, pressing against it and moving in all directions.

26/ Polish the outer side of the ring, as shown in the picture, moving it to avoid marks being caused by excessive contact with the disc.

27/ There are many different sizes and types of felt wheels. To polish the gemstone setting, use a round disc.

28/ A brush with coarse black hairs is very useful for polishing round shapes, but it will be necessary to keep loading it with fresh abrasive.

29

29/ Here, an abrasive brush has been used to polish the inner part of the bowl, the side of the arm of the ring, and the upper part of the setting.

32

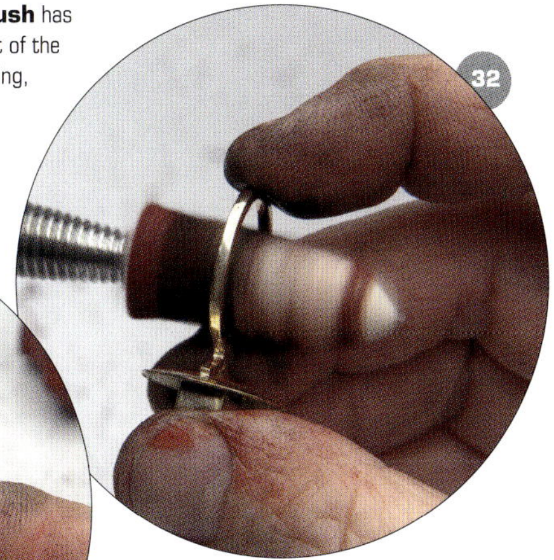

31

30

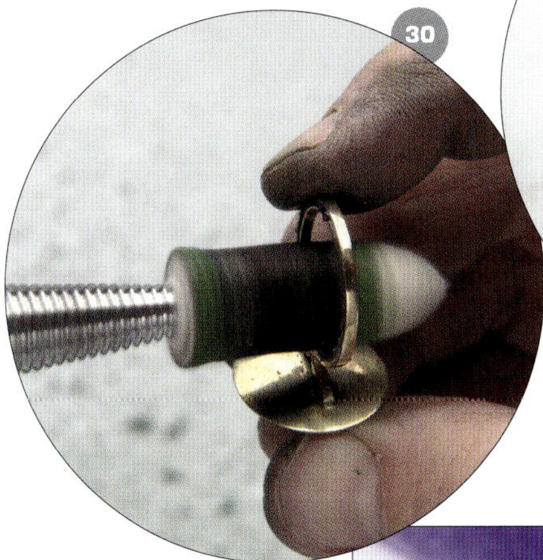

30/ To polish the inside of the ring, a felt of the correct shape is used, moving the ring in all directions. After applying green abrasive paste all over the ring, clean the piece completely before applying the finishing.

32/ The inside of the ring is shined in the same way as it was polished with the abrasive powder.

31/ The same process carried out with the abrasive paste is now repeated using the finishing paste. On this occasion, and when dealing with gold, it is advisable to use red jeweler's rouge paste.

33/ Lastly, shine the ring by applying paste to a stitched cotton pad to obtain the maximum shine for the metal.

33

CodinaOrfebres. Ring with tourmaline.

Fibula of the Kabyle: *Abzim* (Karim Oukid)

The jewelry of the Kabyle has a very important symbolic, cultural and social content that is embedded in the wide repertoire of shapes and designs of the *amazigh* cultural heritage. What follows are instructions for making an *abzim* (an abstract representation of a scorpion), a type of fibula designed to be worn on clothes.

The process shows the basic techniques of the jewelry of the Kabyle: *borsade* filigree, the creation of *cloisonné* filigree patterns, the application of colors and their symbology, the particular way of heating enamels, the preparation of settings, and the polishing of coral and how to set it.

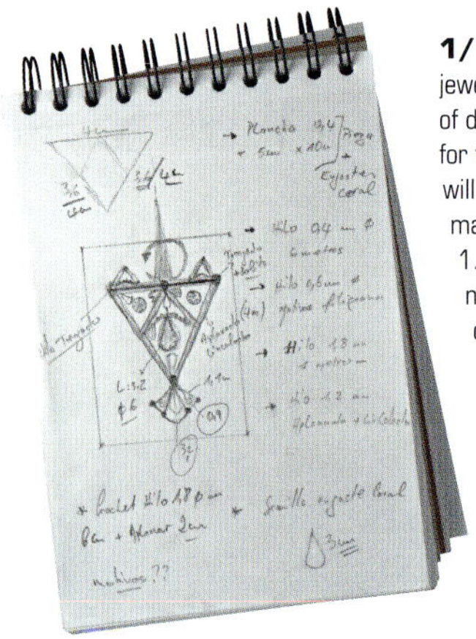

1/ The first step for any jewelry work of the Kabyle consists of defining the design: the spaces for the coral and all the wires that will form part of the object are marked out. Wire of 0.4, 0.6, 1.2, 1.8, and 0.4 mm plate are needed, as well as small pieces of red coral.

2/ The wire must be completely annealed, so it can be twisted and flattened correctly. To do this, tie one end of the wire to a bench vise and the other to a hand drill. Then, wind the two wires until an even wire in the shape of a spiral is formed.

3/ To smooth the wire and leave it completely straight, anneal it, and then stretch it by pulling one of the ends firmly.

4/ On a 04 mm plate, cut three previously annealed, twisted wires of equal length. Dampen in liquid solder and place them in the shape of an equilateral triangle.

5/ Place solder in the form of small squares on top of the wire and apply a reductive flame all over until it begins to melt the silver wire and the plate supporting it.

6

6/ On a round wire, previously flattened in the rolling mill, use a die to make the decoration as shown in the picture.

7/ Now cut three equal parts of the same wire and place them inside the sides of the triangle, making sure they fit well, especially at the ends.

7

9

10

9/ Cut small pieces of twisted wire, which need to be completely straight. To do this, press on them at the same time as rolling them with the opposite end of some tongs on the steel die.

10/ These small wires form an inner triangle inside the structure, which must be soldered in the manner seen previously.

8

8/ Place solder on the upper part and fuse it, with the help of a punch or a bar of steel, to ensure good soldering between the wire and the plate.

11/ The other decorative elements, in the form of teardrops, flowers, and circles, are made in the same way, by bending single or double wires, twisted with various pliers or with different sized presses.

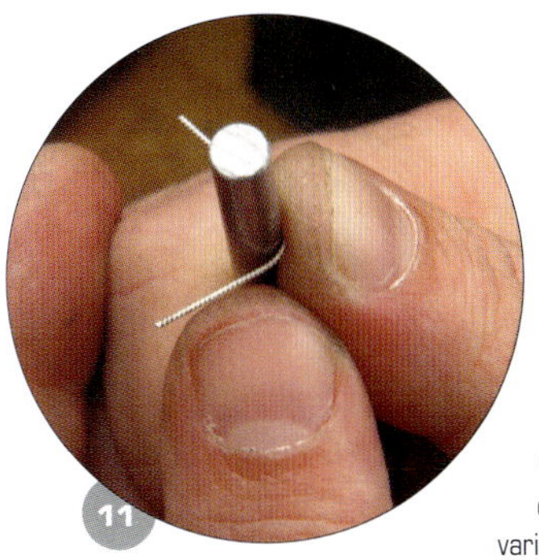

11

12/ Continue the design, dampening the various wires with liquid solder and placing them on top of the plate. Then, secure them with a little heat, apply the solder, and solder together.

12

13/ Each time heat is applied, it is necessary to press the wires onto the plate, thus ensuring that the solder flows correctly between the wires and the plate.

14/ After soldering, the plate tends to bend, making it necessary to tap the structure softly on a steel die.

15/ Once the structure is stripped and dry, place the rest of the decorative elements in the form of drops and small circles of twisted wire.

16/ Place more solder on the wires and apply heat again with the blow torch.

17/ The settings for the coral are made by cutting an indented edge on a 0.4 mm plate with the help of a triangular file. Then they are bent into the shape of a teardrop, ensuring a correct fit inside the structure where they will be placed.

18/ When soldering, a reductive, uniform flame must be applied to cover the whole piece.

19/ Place the settings in position. At the same time, various silver jump rings will also have been melted on a charcoal brick to make small balls that will be placed on the joints of the wires as decorative elements.

20/ Once all the elements are soldered, cut the excess plate off the upper part with scissors.

21/ The clasp is constructed from a round wire of 1.8 mm forged at the end and cut, as shown in the picture.

22/ The other part of the clasp is made by bending a piece of the same wire and soldering two small balls of silver at each end. It is advisable to solder the second ball after inserting it in the soldered ring of the structure.

23/ Solder the end of the clasp onto the upper part of the fibula, and solder two decorated rings on its upper and lower parts, to be able to insert the clasp through the upper ring. Finish by cutting the shape of the piece with scissors and going around the outside with different files.

24/ When the soldering work is finished, strip the piece, then, when it is clean and dry, dampen the enamel. Blue, yellow, and green are the characteristic colors of the jewelry of the Kabyle. Load the paintbrush with enamel and, with an up and down motion, introduce each color into each segment in order.

25/ When the piece has been enameled, let it dry and place it on a steel grid to melt the enamel.

26/ **With the blow torch,** and on the lower part of the fibula, begin to heat the piece in a uniform manner until the enamel flows. It is totally heated when there is a light sheen on the surface. Then remove the flame and let it cool on a refractory brick.

27/ If the heat has been applied correctly, the fibula will not have oxidized.

28/ Good quality coral should be chosen. Those shown here are red, a symbol of protection against the evil eye and spells in the amazigh culture.

29/ Cut the coral with a diamond disc, which must be constantly cooled in water. Continue the main cuts until they fit the size of the setting.

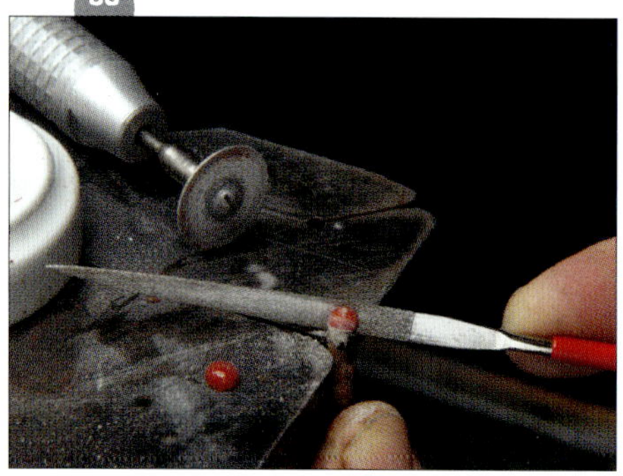

30/ To cut the coral better, it has been fixed to the end of a wooden stick with adhesive. With a dampened diamond file, it is given the shape of a cabochon. It is then polished and shined with the polisher.

31/ Now put the fibula in silver oxide to oxidize it.

32

32/ Polish the silver in the polisher and shine with the help of different tools in the rotary tool.

33

33/ The polished fibula, with coral shaped and properly polished using jeweler's rouge.

34

34/ Place the coral in the setting, where a piece of dampened paper has been placed.

35

35/ With a flat tool, press on the triangular points of the setting against the gemstone until it fits into the setting.

Karim Oukid. ***Abzim.*** **Traditional Kabyle fibula made in silver, enamel, and red coral.**

Gallery

Akiko Kurihara

(15 m) long necklace made of silver from 1000 letter "g" pieces, each weighing a gram and with a total weight of 1 kg.

Enric Majoral

18k gold ring made from a cut plate that was then formed and given texture.

Inés Sobreira

Brooch made in pure silver and different colors of silicone.

Stefano Marchetti

Brooch made by combining different precious metals.

Carmen Amador

Brooch made with pearls, synthetic ruby, gold, and silver. The artist develops small poetic compositions from an entire universe of small objects, some by themselves invaluable.

Jlla and Martin Kaufmann

ecklace made from a sheet f 21 mm forged yellow gold.

Abril Ribera and Roc Majoral

8k gold necklace with rubies nd black nylon wire.

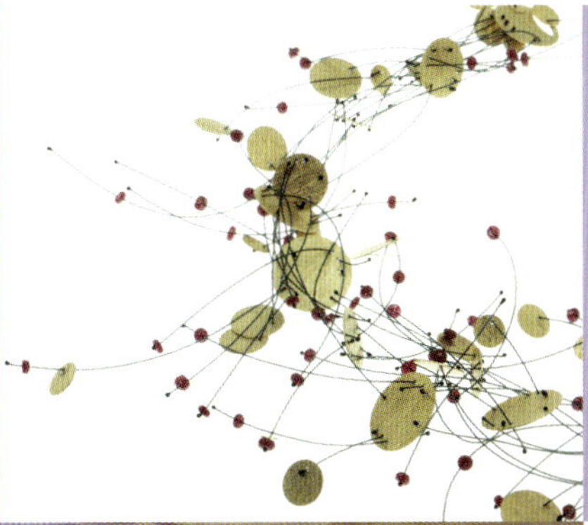

Liliana Guerreiro

Silver and gold ring made with filigree mesh.

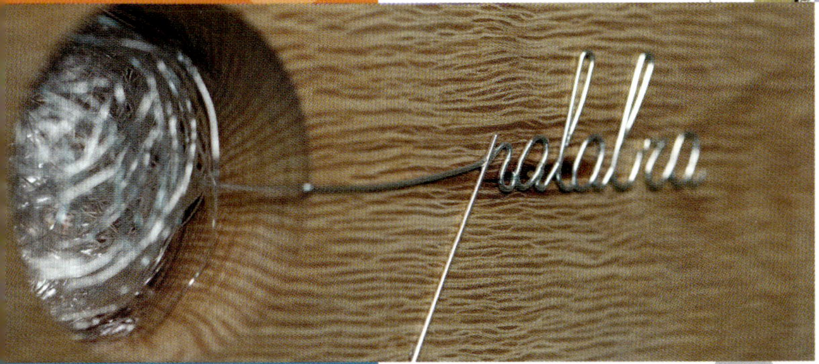

Karim Oukid

Kabyle fibula (*Thabzimth*) made in silver. Symbolic piece that restores an ideal of the thoughts and feelings of the Berber culture of the Kabyle with a particular style and language.

Luis Méndez

Detail of the sculpture Palabra-Sentido. The metal has been worked in traditional filigree.

Acknowledgments

Basic Metal Jewelry Techniques: A Masterclass has no other goal than to provide some basic knowledge and inspiration for those people who are attracted to the trade and some processes that are too many for just one person to provide. For this reason, I would like to give heartfelt thanks for the collaboration of all those who have generously given their work use in this book: Enric Majoral, Abril Ribera and Roc Majoral, Ana Cardim, Akiko Kurihara, Carmen Amador, Daniel Fàbregues, Ulla and Martin Kaufmann, Inés Sobreira, Stefano Marchetti, Liliana Guerreiro, Luis Méndez, and Diego Bisso. I also give my sincere thanks to all the artists who have unselfishly sent me their work but, for reasons of space, it has been impossible to include them.

I would like to give special thanks to Karim Oukid for his enthusiasm in making the Kabyle fibula, for contributing to disseminating a process, and for showing a small part of the culture of the Kabyle, which is a special interest of mine.

I also thank Leinajoya for its kindness in letting me use and photograph all the material that I have needed for this book.

Lastly, I thank, for their patience and professionalism, the two people with whom I have worked most closely on making this book: the photographer Joan Soto and the editor Cristina Vilella.